BEGINNERS
FENG SHUI

Easy tips to enhance everyday living

BY

MICHELE VOS-CASTLE

Thank you for stepping into the transforming world of Feng Shui. May you be empowered, educated, enlightened and inspired by your home and environment.

What a journey. Blessings love and thanks to all the loves, friends, clients, students and especially my world outside of Feng Shui my children Shelby, Zane, and Felix. Thank you all for coming into my world for the experiences, education, lessons, and support throughout my journey. Without all I would not be who I am. We are all teachers and students; on the chaotic rollercoaster we call life!

Michele Vos-Castle

REVIEWS

"I have been following Michele's Feng Shui advice for over 12 years She is an amazing, very professional person with many of her predications being very accurate."
Dot O'Sullivan

"Michele has a wealth of knowledge of all aspects of Feng Shui, which she shares with generosity and clarity. She interprets the Chinese astrology charts of each member of the household with great insight and intuitive understanding. Michele is always empathetic to the needs and circumstances of her clients and has helped me and my family tremendously over the many years we have made use of her services. I highly recommend Michele and her work!"
Annie Vorster

"Michele is a true master of Feng Shui. I have had her involved with my own homes and my workplace's for about 16 or 17 years now. She is a pleasure to work with and knows so much about Feng Shui and how to remedy all situations. Having Feng Shui in my life has helped the energy of my family and workplace, and make them amazing places to want to be – you can feel the calmness and the energy flowing. I am hooked, I love the beginning of every new year, to see what has changed. I love the Bazi Charts you get too, so many interesting things about life and yourself."
Ann Meney

"Great experience with Michele. Very approachable, polite, and friendly. Michele has a lot of Feng Shui knowledge. I feel that I can still ask her questions even after she has completed my consultation and report. Will continue with Michele for all future Feng Shui and interior design matters."
Mary Valentina

"Since I first met Michele from Complete Feng Shui eight years ago, she has guided me on energetically restoring my house's virtues, found me a landscape artist to design the Garden of Eden of my dreams and sailed me onto the sweet shores of fulfilling romance. She is my go-to guru and a master of her craft."
Monica Wood

"We have known Michele for over 12 years. Always very happy with the Feng Shui readings she does for us yearly, we often refer to and use as guidance throughout each year. Michele has helped us with the purchase of our homes. Happily, highly recommend Michele when you need a Feng Shui master for your house, office, and guidance yearly to get you through the year – year after year fan. Michele is very warm, approachable and brings a beautiful energy within her presence."
Aria & Michael Van Uffelen

"Michele Castle is an amazing Feng Shui master and has done a very detailed informative book for my home and family. The detailed charts and reports gave us great insight, her amazing experience and explanations help guide us with what the energy is bringing with the year and elements. It has helped us be best prepared, even for the best Feng Shui for our business and money as well. I am grateful for Michele's guidance, and I trust her and highly recommend her to my family and friends for her in-depth Feng Shui knowledge."
Bass Tadros

"I have been fortunate enough to have been introduced to Michele and Feng Shui at least 6 years ago. It came about around the trials and tribulations I was having with the building and surroundings I lived and continue to live in. Well, I took on the recommendation to have her check the place out and was pleasantly surprised at her findings and cures and hence allowing peace and harmony to return to my home again. I have completed some courses with Michele and am amazed at how knowledgeable, intuitive, and magical she is... brilliant Feng Shui master in my books. I continue to use her for annual assessment of energy flows etc for my home and other aspects of my life. Love her work and her as a professional being that she is. I highly recommend Michele as a Feng Shui expert and teacher."
Bhavna Mistry

"Michele is always helpful and willing to advise what works best for everyone in our household. We have engaged her service for over 10 years now on property purchase and annual readings. She is always friendly and so easy to work with. Highly recommend her service."
Frank Walsh

Published by Complete Feng Shui
Mobile: +61 421 116 799
Email: michele@completefengshui.com
www.completefengshui.com

Author: Michele Vos-Castle
Title: Beginners Feng Shui
ISBN: 978-0-6452137-0-6 (Print)
          978-0-6452137-2-0 (eBook)

Platinum Member of the Association of Feng Shui Consultants (AFSC)
Recognised Feng Shui Training Institution by the AFSC

 completefengshui   @completefengshui

CONTENTS

MY STORY

You may question what led a young mum of three towards a life governed by Feng Shui. A roller coaster comes to mind as a perfect description.

I was raised by a builder and lived in Belair, Cobar, Bowen, and Echuca. Moving around I experienced many different housing arrangements. I went from prestigious Belair to a home on stilts that rocked with movement on a cold front. One home stood out amongst the lot, the home of my Aunty Nikki. Working in a furniture shop in Subiaco, her home décor was bursting with patterns, fabrics, and textures. I wanted a home just like it and aspired to the realm of Interior Design. I studied the profession which led to architectural drafting, I was engrossed by the impact that design elements played and started analysing my life and the countless houses I had once called home. Reviewing the shifts in life and luck while in each household.

Over 20 years ago I discovered Feng Shui. Like many I read about the subject and researched its momentum and interest in the west. As friends had their homes healed my Feng Shui curiosity flourished. A Feng Shui consultant came to my home, with pen in hand. I followed her around as she instructed on colours, furniture placement and an assortment of symbolism. Red needed to be removed from a wall, furniture directions needed adjustment, Jade and Cumquat plants were to be placed at doors, mirrors and pictures re-homed, salt went in certain spots, crystals hung to redirect energy and the list went on. The thought of a change in luck stimulated interest and desire. I was in a tailspin - amazed - this was an exciting new venture and a great excuse for an upskill and unbeknown to me also a change in my life direction.

I am the Chinese Zodiac animal Rooster. It was important that I understood WHY I could not have a particular wall red, WHY I needed to place salt and crystals in certain pockets and WHY I was affected by mirrors or the symbolism of artwork. There were a lot of WHYs and so my Feng Shui journey started.

I read any books relating to the topic. Every wall was painted, and furniture textures, colours and placements were altered to follow Feng Shui principles. My home became warm and inviting with lots of energy and light. My living space looked and felt great. Family and friends liked the energy and requested I help them achieve similar outcomes and with that my journey intensified. I began investing in courses under well-recognised Feng Shui masters. Wanting to really understand the many levels and influences of energy that was Feng Shui, the 'Art of placement and manipulation of energy'. Feng Shui as an art just clicked, it made sense being more mathematical, analytical, and practical approach.

Over the past 20 years I have navigated and now understand the multi- layered science and practice of Feng Shui.

I have taught Feng Shui, Chinese Astrology and Metaphysical Studies for the Asian Studies unit at Curtin University. Worked extensively on interiors, renovations, and with emerging businesses and established enterprises. Through many years of practising and consulting I became an author and public speaker and now bring my wealth of knowledge and experience to this new Feng Shui series. You will start with simple steps and tips to begin your own journey and learn to master the energy of space within your home and environment.

This is quite simply the book I wish had started my Feng Shui adventure! Welcome to the transforming world of Feng Shui!

INTRODUCTION

Feng Shui is an ancient body of knowledge which originated thousands of years ago in China. It is the ancient art and science of placement; to bring about a balance between people and their environment - to enrich living. It means 'wind' and 'water', which in Chinese culture are associated with good health. We have all experienced Feng Shui in our lives - whether we are aware of it, or not.

Feng Shui works on the basis that there are energy currents - known as 'Chi' - that flow through the home. When these energy currents flow through the home, the atmosphere is vibrant and positive, but when they are blocked, negative energies and obstructions are present. These stagnate and may cause damage to the health and attitudes of the people living there; creating arguments, sickness, misfortune, bad luck, setbacks and difficulties. The blockage of positive energy may stem from many origins including incorrect placement of furniture or objects, poor room orientation, an unsupportive surrounding landscape, harmful Earth energies or negative energy from past residents.

Naturally, our destiny and fortune are also influenced by factors other than our homes. However, none of the problems resulting from poor Feng Shui are inevitable and insurmountable. Its principles can be applied to your home or place of work, and Feng Shui promises that once you create balance and harmony you will increase your peace, security, prosperity, happiness, health, love and luck.

The art of Feng Shui is extensive with many schools to choose from to adapt its principles. There is an abundance of information available, and admittedly, it can be overwhelming. The aim of this book is to give you simple tips, from a combination of the schools, creating balance and harmony that you can apply to your everyday life, and there is a glossary for your reference. Let's begin!

ATTRACT MORE CLARITY
WITH A SUPPORTIVE
NURTURING ENVIRONMENT.

FENG SHUI IN THE HOME

Your home is an important aspect of your life, and creating balance and harmony within your home places you in a steadfast position on the road to good health, wealth and prosperity.

ENTRANCE WAYS

The main door is one of the three important factors when assessing the Feng Shui of a home. It is the threshold between Yin (internal) and Yang (external), and therefore acts as the 'mouth' where energy enters the property. A good main door ensures that the entire building receives a healthy amount of energy. Too large a doorway will allow Chi to escape from your home. If this is a problem for you, it can be easily counteracted by placing a Windchime outside the door. This will also discourage Sha (negative energy) from entering your home. Too small a doorway will not allow enough Chi to enter the home, but placing a mirror on either side of the door will help to fix the problem.

It is important the flow of Chi, from the front to the back of your home, is not hindered. It is also best to have it flow through in a meandering path and not a direct line. If the back door can be seen from the front door, Chi can flow straight through your home without circulating. Placing a large potted plant or a screen in between the two will break up the straight lines and help to deflect Chi.

The entrance hall is most auspicious in terms of Feng Shui, as it is the place where one might pause upon entering or leaving the home, thus being energised by the Chi that flows through it. Entrance halls that have no windows or doors leading from them, or are enclosed in some way, can cause Chi to stagnate. Mirrors or a ceiling fan, or a small water fountain may solve this problem.

STAIRWAYS

Poorly positioned stairways can cause problems in the way they deflect Chi. A stairway directly opposite the front door will allow most of the Chi to rush through and up to the next level causing the ground floor to starve. Mirrors, Windchimes, potted plants and screens are all effective ways of slowing down the movement of Chi in this case.

If you have an open stairway that uses risers as opposed to filled in steps, it will not allow enough Chi to flow to the next floor. Placing plants beneath the stairs will help to deflect Chi upwards, thus allowing the flow to continue. A skylight over the stairs will also help improve the situation.

Stairways that curve along their path are ideal, however, if there is too sharp a bend, we solve this dilemma with the use of mirrors or plants.

LOUNGE ROOM

In Feng Shui the lounge room is considered to be the heart of the home because it is the place reserved for relaxation, conversation, interaction and relationships.

The lounge room should be in the South side of the home or should face South. West is also a good outlook and it should have a pleasant view. If the view from your lounge room has harsh lines or angles such as a neighbouring home or a city skyline, try breaking the lines up with large plants.

Your lounge room should be square or rectangular in shape and the furniture should be placed so as to break opposing straight lines. This will allow Chi to flow gently through a room. Alcoves and dead areas can be broken up with the placement of plants, large items of furniture or fish tanks.

Flat ceilings are best for promoting the flow of Chi. If, however, you have a sloped ceiling or exposed beams you should use Bamboo Flutes as a remedy.

Many lounge rooms are adjacent to dining rooms or kitchens and in these cases it's best to have a visual barrier placed between them such as a screen or large plants. If you have doors in between, try to keep them closed.

Seating in your lounge room should be placed in a way that breaks up direct pathways. Avoid placing the back of a lounge chair or settee directly against a wall. This will break the lines and secret arrows which produce Sha energy. There should also be an even number of seats in the room. The most comfortable seat in the room should be reserved for a guest and should never have its back facing a door.

The lounge room should have an open and inviting feel to it. Avoid overcrowding the room with furniture. If necessary, remove the least used items in the room to achieve this feeling. An area that has stagnant Chi is best remedied with an aquarium or a television. The placement of flowers or potted plants are also effective cures for these areas.

Colour your lounge room wisely. Don't use harsh colours or colours that oppose the furniture or artwork. Where possible, derive the colours from your artwork to help create a harmony between the two. Soft pastels are always good. Before making a final decision on colour, check out the symbolic definition for them in my colour chapter on page 22.

DINING ROOM

The seating arrangements for the family dining table are based on the order of the trigrams of the Bagua (which is a Feng Shui school). The ideal shape for your table is the octagon as this represents the eight sided Bagua. However, tables of this shape are difficult to come by and not always practical. A round table is said by some experts to be 'as good', symbolising earth and stability. If your table is rectangular or square, the placing of an octagonal centrepiece or placemats is good Feng Shui.

When arranging furniture in the dining room ensure that chairs don't restrict doorways. There should be ample space for guests to walk around the table without having to manoeuvre around chairs or other furniture.

There should be an even number of dining chairs and remember to seat an honoured guest facing the doorway. Dining chairs with a horseshoe shaped back are ideal Feng Shui as this shape represents the 'Dragon embracing the Tiger'.

If your dining room has no windows, a chandelier or a ceiling fan will assist the flow of Chi. Always use soft, even lighting in the dining room, as well as soft colours such as shades of green or yellow.

KITCHEN

The kitchen is the second of the three important factors when assessing Feng Shui of a home.

It is sometimes described as the 'soul of the house'. It is where the food that nourishes all the residents is cleaned, prepared, cooked and stored. It is also the part of the home that both affects and is influenced by the mother energy of the home. This area embodies all the important elements that bind members of the household together - love, unity, patience and compassion.

Two important elements feature in the kitchen; the stove is considered the Fire element, and the sink and refrigerator are considered the Water element. Ideally, don't place the stove either next to, or directly opposite the sink or refrigerator - this is because of the incompatibility of Water and Fire.

The stove is crucial because this is where food is cooked - when food is cooked, it transforms from one state (Yin) to another (Yang). A stove located in a prosperous sector of the house ensures the occupants are well nourished and healthy.

Let's look at the stove positioning in more detail:
- The stove should be positioned so as to avoid the cook standing with her/his back to a doorway. A mirror, or any highly reflective kitchen appliance, placed above the stove will counteract this problem by providing a reflection so the cook cannot be taken by surprise. Good lighting and ventilation by the stove will reduce the influence of Sha
- The stove should be at least one metre away from the sink. This energises the stove making the food that is cooked in it auspicious for the family
- The stove should not be in the North West sector. This is called 'Fire at Heaven's Gate' and brings bad luck to the breadwinner, causing the head of the household to lose their job and money by the Fire. This is because the North West is the corner of your house that represents the father, and it also represents the place where heaven energy (which is spiritual energy) pours into the home
- The stove should not face the main door or any bedroom door
- The stove should not be directly under an exposed overhead beam
- The stove should not be placed directly under a toilet on the floor above
- The stove should not directly face a toilet door
- A toilet next to a kitchen produces Sha. Keeping the door closed and the toilet lid down will help
- Your kitchen should always have sufficient lighting, and be airy and spacious
- Kitchens should never be located in the middle of the home and they are better positioned nearer the back rather than the front
- White is the preferred colour for kitchens. It symbolises purity and therefore promotes good health from well prepared (pure) food. Cutlery should not be stored in a stagnant area as the negative influence of sharp objects will serve to cut your health. Place them in a drawer nearest to the doorway or window.

BEDROOM

The bedroom is the third of the three important factors when assessing Feng Shui of a home. Bedrooms are where most of our time is physically spent to replenish our bodies (Yin) after a hard day's work (Yang). As such, the location of the bedrooms directly affects the health and emotional well-being of its occupants. Generally, a well-supported bedroom is one that 'sees' a hill or higher ground externally – this is where the energy is stable and sentimental (versus fast-moving and aggressive).

Adults will benefit more from a bedroom facing West into gentle rays of the setting sun, whereas children will reap the rewards of the bedroom facing East towards the invigorating morning rays. Those with no children should decide which is best for them, be it a deeper, more relaxing sleep (West) or the vitality and motivation of morning (East).

The bed should not be placed so that the occupant's feet face a doorway. This is the way the deceased are carried from a room. Neither should your bed directly face a window as the glare attracts Sha energy.

A bedroom beside the living room is good Feng Shui and in the case of a two-storey home, directly above a lounge room is best.

The bedroom is a room for relaxation and the colours you choose should be peaceful and tranquil. Too vibrant a colour will excite Chi making it difficult to rest. This also applies to the lighting in your bedroom – try lowering the wattage of the globes used in this room. Colours such as blue and black represent the Water element, and this promotes bad Feng Shui luck in the bedroom – which is why water features should never be placed in bedrooms; as well as not using water beds or pillows. The best colours for the bedroom are of pink and red hues as they promote romance and love.

Mirrors shouldn't be placed in bedrooms as they deplete your personal energy. If you have mirrors in your bedroom which can't be removed, try covering them up with pictures or draping fabric over them.

BATHROOM

A bathroom facing North is ideal as this direction is associated with the Water element. The colours blue and black are favoured in a bathroom for their significance to water. Great care should be taken to ensure safety. Sharp objects and non-slip surfaces are things to consider, as are the proximity of water to electrical outlets. Ensure that from the bath or shower the door can be seen, a carefully placed mirror can help prevent the bather from being taken by surprise.

Bathrooms and toilets are used for hygiene. These rooms can actually pollute Chi, so we want to encourage the speedy flow of Chi here. The aim is to wash away the pollution and replace the Chi as quickly as possible. Breezy windows, mirrors and Feng Shui crystals will assist the flow of Chi.

As we are encouraging the flow of Chi in this area, we need to be careful not to drain Chi from a wealth area such as a home office or study nearby.

TOILET

The toilet gets a lot of bad press in Feng Shui as it's said to flush away wealth, relationships and other good things in life. While some readily place little trinkets in their washrooms in hope of 'preventing money from being flushed away', others go as far as to structurally relocate their toilets to another section of the house.

Which begs the question: Where is it best for toilets to go, if any? It becomes a problem when the main door of a house is directly aligned with the bathroom door. When energy enters the property through the main door, it flows straight into the toilet, thus, not allowing it to meander and flow throughout the entire home. As such, occupants will not be able to benefit from any energy that enters the property.

This is especially true when the distance after entering the main door to the toilet door, is less than three metres apart. In the long run, this condition depletes the positive life force (Yang) energy of the people in the house. As long as it is kept clean, there should not be any Feng Shui fuss about toilets. After all, no one can live without a toilet, so it helps to apply common sense.

STUDY

It is important to keep this room tidy and uncluttered as failing to do so will produce Sha. As this is a room where we require creativity and contemplation we must do all we can to produce Chi. It's helpful to have an area with no shelving where a comfortable high-backed chair can be placed for quiet contemplation. The Chinese refer to this area as the Ming T'ang. Placing a picture symbolising water behind the chair will help encourage the flow of creative energy.

Place the desk so that the window is to the left of the seating position and so that the door can be seen from the desk. Don't allow the occupant's back to face the door. If there is no window available put a mirror or picture in its place.

Take care to remedy the view of threatening elements from the window with plants. Bamboo is a plant grown in very harsh conditions and symbolises good fortune, thus making them ideal for placement in the home office, study or wealth area. Any sharp leaved plants are good Feng Shui in this area as they are believed to deter harmful influences. Further on in this book, we'll look at more tips for education luck.

GARDEN

The size of your garden is irrelevant when it comes to planning and layout.

The garden is the Yin and the home is the Yang, so the overall effect of your garden should convey the balance of Yin and Yang. There should be a balance of straight lines and angles. Flower beds and curved paths can be used to counterpoint and balance the straight lines of a house.

Balance can be achieved in the garden with the use of contrasting textures such as the roughness of rocks joining the smooth surface of water. The contrast of rocks and water also represents the balance of stillness (rocks) and movement (water) and the harmony of humans and nature. The size of your garden may make it difficult to include a watercourse. This can be overcome with the simple addition of a birdbath or fountain.

PAVING

Entrance ways off the street, or through your garden, to the front door will determine the qualities of Chi that flow into your home. Therefore, it is important to have curved pathways or garden beds. Breaking up the direction of pavers to allow curved lines will also help. It's good Feng Shui to reduce Sha when using paving, by avoiding the use of overtly straight lines. Curved paving stones are best, but straight-edged paving stones laid in curved lines or a herringbone pattern will help break up the edges and encourage Chi. If you have a large existing paved area which is impractical to re-lay, then the careful placement of a table and chairs, or plants according to Feng Shui principles, will enhance the Chi flow. A birdbath, fountain or a small pond along the way will bring balance and also improve the qualities of Chi.

FENCE AND HEDGES

It's ideal Feng Shui for the boundaries of your property to be of curved walls or irregular shaped hedges and flower beds, rather than high, straight fences. If your boundaries are made of high fences they can be easily broken up with flower beds or creeping vines. The principle behind applying Feng Shui to the garden is to ensure that it is balanced within itself and it then balances within the home. Remember, the components of your garden such as pathways, garden beds, fences and retaining walls, all play an important role in balancing Feng Shui.

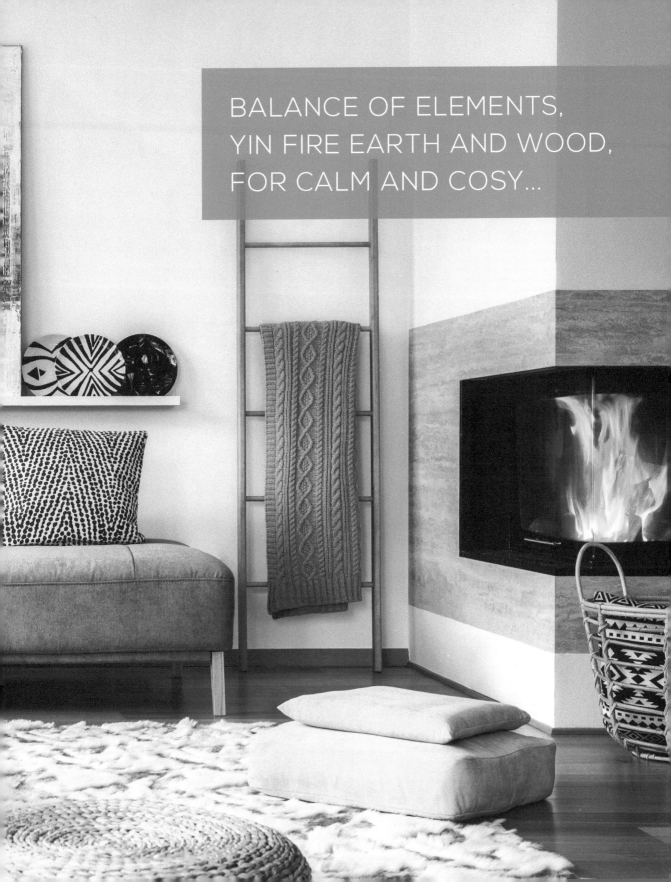

BALANCE OF ELEMENTS,
YIN FIRE EARTH AND WOOD,
FOR CALM AND COSY...

THE USE OF COLOUR

Colour permeates the world and everybody is influenced by it. It is believed that colour is energy that vibrates in the same way as heat, sound, and radio waves. It denotes our personalities, dreams and desires. It can drain energy or inspire vitality, help or hinder attitudes and emotions. You can empower your life through selecting the right colours for your home; and improve key areas of your life from health to love, and to wealth. Colour can be used to make real changes that will affect you immediately.

Your home is your personal sanctuary from the stresses and strains of the world. It is at home where you spend time and can relax, and time spent at home is invaluable for rebalancing your energies.

Choosing the right hues and tones for each room in your home can create positive energy. We all react individually to the energy of colour because it vibrates at different frequencies and creates a reaction in all of us. The colour that emanates from our walls and decor has the power to make us feel content, calm, or inspired to socialise. Conversely, unsuitable colours may make us unsettled, restless, argumentative, and even cause ill health and loss of wealth.

Feng Shui uses colours in specific ways for such things as bringing harmony to an area, increasing or decreasing the amount of energy in a room, controlling detrimental energy flow, and guiding energy around a home or building.

Have you ever walked into a room and immediately felt relaxed and at peace? This will often happen in a blue room because this colour sends out calming, short energy-waves. In an orange room, however, the warmth and vibrancy of this colour has longer wavelengths that may make you feel refreshed and revitalised. Let's take a closer look at the different energy each colour emits and which rooms they best suit.

RED

Red is the colour for activating passion, love, romance, and it energises sexual desire. It is a magnificent colour to use for maintaining your love relationship. It is also the main colour for bringing joy and excitement in your home. It is ideal to be used in your living areas such as dining room, lounge room and kitchen; and your main bedroom. In your living areas it will bring much daily joy, and in your bedroom it will serve to increase and maintain passion, love and romance with a special partner.

In Chinese culture red is the colour of luck and happiness, and it is the marriage colour in India.

Avoid red if you're prone to insomnia or anxiety, or if there is too much activity happening in your life.

ORANGE

Orange is a happy, vibrant and social colour. It brings much activity, cheer and social occasions to the home. The energy it creates is of lively conversations and gatherings. It is a fun-loving colour.

Like red, it can be used in your living areas and bedroom, however, it's not as intense as red. It's ideal in your living areas rather than red if you want a moderation of activity. It is less affecting than red but still inspiring. Its use in the main bedroom is still affective but will soften sexual desire, passion and romance. An earthy orange colour is best for the bedroom and mixing it in with red hues is a fantastic colour combination.

Avoid orange if you're wishing to create a quiet area.

YELLOW

Yellow is a very warm, uplifting and happy colour. Its energy gives off a welcoming feeling. It's a very mentally stimulating colour and therefore can activate intelligence in individuals.

It is a fantastic colour for use in the living room, dining room and kitchen. It's an active and social colour which brings a sunny disposition to the home's occupants and visitors. If using it in the main bedroom, a pale, earthy tone is best. Bright sunflower yellows are perfect in a child's bedroom.

Yellow should be avoided in cases of nervousness and anxiety.

GREEN

Green is the colour of growth and vibrancy. It represents abundance, nature, renewal and freshness. It is a very relaxing and tranquil colour with calming and balancing effects. It's a nourishing colour for health and activates a healing throughout your whole body receiving vibrations from nature. It radiates peace and new beginnings.

It is predominantly beneficial when used in a bathroom as it activates fresh energy, however, it is suitable for any room. It's recommended that several differing shades of green are used in combination with each other as this maximises its effects.

Due to green's balancing nature it should be used more often than not.

BLUE

Blue is the colour of calmness, peace and tranquillity. It is a relaxing colour and it heals and soothes the soul. It offers spiritual attunement, communication and honesty. It's a dependable colour that offers security.

Like green, blue is one of the best colours to use in a bathroom. It should never be used in a main bedroom.

Blue should be avoided if depression is prone.

PURPLE

Purple signifies nobility, abundance and royalty. It is often related to spirituality and intuition as its energy is calming and soothing. It's best used in moderation throughout the home such as with ornaments rather than full wall colours, as it gives off a very high vibration.

It is the ideal colour for use in a room dedicated to mediation or healing. It can also be used in small amounts in your main bedroom for a softer romantic touch.

Purple should be avoided if you are looking to increase activity in your life.

BLACK

Black is a mysterious and secretive colour - it is unknown and endless. It's an introspective colour and denotes complexity, power, style and modernism. It's helpful for the use of career, skills and knowledge.

It is a colour that is best used as in small amounts with decor items throughout the home. Black is never to be used in a main bedroom.

Avoid black if depression is prone, or if there is difficulty in expressing oneself.

WHITE

White is the colour of new beginnings, purity, clarity and innocence. Its energy emitted is of hope and freeness. There is often a feeling of cleanliness and freshness when one walks into a white room. It is also a spiritual colour.

It is a great colour to use in areas of creativity especially for children, and a fantastic colour to use in the bathroom due to its symbolism of purity.

White should be avoided when feeling overwhelmed.

GREY

Grey is a quiet, calm and detached colour. It is deemed as conservative and boring, and can have a draining effect on energy levels. However, it is also considered as a sophisticated colour and can be useful for creativity.

Grey is best used in moderation as an accessory colour only.

Avoid grey in abundance if you're prone to depression.

BROWN

Brown is the colour of stability, strength and reliability. It is a nurturing and motherly colour offering comfort and a grounded feeling.

Use brown in your living areas for best results.

Avoid brown if you are wishing to expand any area of your life.

PINK

Pink is the universal colour of unconditional love. It is romantic, gentle, soothing and peaceful. Its feminine energy is soft and nurturing. It is the ideal colour for igniting love and romance in a special relationship.

It can be used freely in your home, however, it is best suited abundantly in the main bedroom.

Pink should be avoided if you are wishing to create more masculine energy.

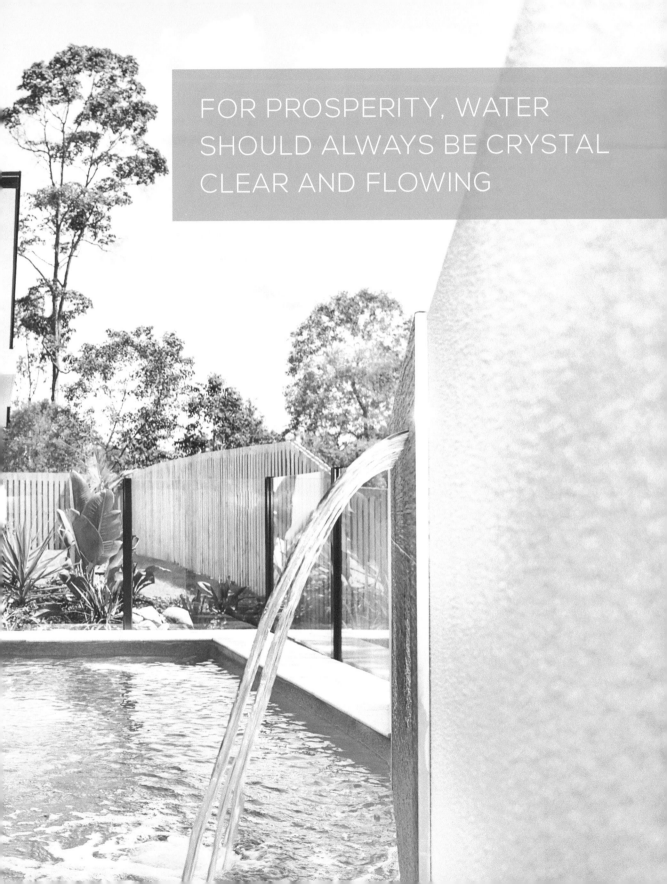

FOR PROSPERITY, WATER
SHOULD ALWAYS BE CRYSTAL
CLEAR AND FLOWING

EIGHT SIMPLE TIPS TO IMPROVE YOUR LIFE

TIP ONE

REMOVE THE CLUTTER

This is the one single problem that I see the most and it is also one of the easiest to remedy. Clutter can cause stagnant energy to accumulate; causing people to feel drained, tired and lethargic. When I walk into a home and look around, I can usually tell by seeing heaps of clutter if the occupants are experiencing difficulties, challenges and issues. We seem to come from a generation of hoarders, taught never to get rid of anything. We think we might need it someday, only to have it sitting there for years, taking up space and collecting dust. So, have a good sort through and clear out the clutter, you will improve the energy levels and work levels; and productivity will increase to no end. There is also a wise saying; 'To make way for the new to come into your life, you need to get rid of the old'.

TIP TWO

GET A WATER FEATURE

Water features are a popular Feng Shui initiative as they are great for improving wealth. They come in myriad of forms. You can have a table top or wall water feature, fish tank or bowl, a fish pond and of course a swimming pool. There are, however, a few placement rules and we'll look at water features in more depth in the next chapter.

TIP THREE

USE A MONEY FROG ORNAMENT

A simple way to help increase wealth coming in to the home is with a Feng Shui three-legged Money Frog (also known as a Moon Frog) – he brings in money and opportunities to the home. Place the frog by the front door and ensure his face is pointing going in to the home. If you place him with his face pointing out towards the door, this represents money leaving. The Money Frog comes with a coin in his mouth and it's important the side of the coin with the four Chinese characters (or it may have a stone), is facing up. This is the Yang side which is more active and aggressive, and that's what you want when inviting money in to your home or business. The Yin side, which is the passive side, has two characters on it and should always be facing down.

TIP FOUR

BE AWARE OF MIRROR PLACEMENTS

Never have mirrors opposite your front entrance door. This will bounce any good positive Chi straight back out the door again - it isn't given the chance to meander through the rest of the home (or place of work). Never have a mirror in line with doors or windows. Be careful with mirrors that reflect the bed. For a small child it may create nightmares, for adults it creates irritability, lethargy, tiredness and health issues (some can be serious). A solid bed end will block the mirror. If it's a dressing table mirror, you can cover it with a sheet or table cloth at night. With large robe mirrors, you can either remove or reverse them. If that is not an option, then I suggest installing a curtain to drop down at night or cover the mirror completely with pictures and posters. And if those aren't options, place a Mayan Ball in front of the mirror.

TIP FIVE

GET RID OF CACTI AND DRIED PLANTS

Cacti plants are considered to be exceptionally negative plants as they represent 'poison arrows' which can affect health in a major way. I would recommend removing them completely. Having dried flower arrangements are also exceptionally negative as they have no life and therefore are 'dead'. Having them in your master bedroom can create relationship issues. At a front entrance of a business they can cause financial challenges. Again, I would recommend that you remove them completely and I would suggest having live, colourful plants, and of course fresh flowers are best - just remember to discard them as soon as they die and replace with fresh, new flowers.

TIP SIX

USE JADE AND CUMQUAT PLANTS FOR ABUNDANCE

I recommend, if possible, placing a pair of either Jade or Cumquat plants on either side of your front entrance as they represent abundance. You can also have both of them, but only if you have the space for them as you don't want to be preventing the flow of energy from being able to get through the front door. With Jade plants, if they are growing mad and touch the ground, then you will need to clip them back - don't chop them right back though, or your finances will also suddenly be chopped back.

TIP SEVEN

KEEP BATHROOM AND TOILET DOORS CLOSED

Open bathroom and toilet doors represent money and energy going down the drains. In ancient times these areas were nowhere near the main place of residence. Today, we can see homes with up to three bathrooms and toilets which are inside the home. In some of the newer, modern homes, the ensuites have no doors and the entries are getting wider and more ornate. The obvious solution for those homes with doors on these rooms, is to keep the doors closed at all times. For those that are open, I suggest installing a door of some kind - this can be a proper door, sliding door, sliding blind or screen, or perhaps a curtain. I would also suggest that you get in to the habit of putting the toilet lid down once you have finished. My daughter learnt from an early age to close the toilet lid and doors; telling her it would be her pocket money going down the drain was a great incentive.

TIP EIGHT

SET UP YOUR OFFICE DESK FOR SUCCESS

Whether your office desk is at your place of work or in your home, ensure that it has at least one side up against a wall. Never have it sitting in the middle of the room - this is what we call a 'floating desk' and the result can be no support for the business or person who sits there. If possible, place the desk so that you can see doors and windows. To have your back to a door can cause a person to become tired and lethargic, as well as feel insecure. I would also suggest having your desk so that you have your back to a solid wall with only enough space to get in and out as this places you in a position of authority - the power seat if you like. When you don't have your back to a wall, it can cause you to become vulnerable. If you're not in a position whereby you can move your desk, get a chair with a high back to give you the support - a bit like a throne. Ensure your desk is clear of clutter or you will become unproductive. You can also place a Laughing Buddha on your desk for prosperity.

WATER FEATURES

Water features bring the energy of the Water element, and water is an ancient Feng Shui symbol of wealth and prosperity. They come in many forms and regardless of whether it's a table top or wall water feature, fish tank or bowl, fish pond or swimming pool, there are a few placement rules:

- First of all, ensure the water feature has flowing water. The water needs to be moving and crystal clear as stagnant water will create stagnant finances. Also ensure the flow of water is going towards the home, or your main door or window. If it is an inside water feature ensure the flow is directed into the home. This represents money coming in. The flow must be smooth and strong, but not too fast. The larger the body of water, the more Chi will be retained or accumulated

- Ensure you never let the water become green and murky; this will have a negative impact on your finances and the larger the volume of water the bigger the impact

- If you have a fish pond or tank, eight or nine goldfish is the most auspicious amount to have. Never have fighting fish as this creates conflicts

- The best place to position a water feature is the South East section of your home, garden, or place of work as this is the wealth section. The exception of not placing a water feature in the South East section is if your bathroom or toilet are located there

- Never place a water feature in a bedroom that is being used for sleeping in (including pictures of water and the colours blue and black) as it represents financial losses

- Other Feng Shui areas of association to place your water feature are; East for health and family happiness, and North for career and path in life

- It's advisable to not place a water feature in the South area as it is connected to your fame and reputation, and the energy of it is Fire. Therefore, Water into the Fire element area (South), creates conflicting energy as Water puts out the Fire

- Major landforms and water bodies in your home's vicinity will complicate the placement, it's wise to do further research for best results.

LUCK ENHANCEMENT

12 WAYS TO ENHANCE YOUR CHARISMA AND INNER STRENGTH

Learn how to improve your finances, career and confidence with this series of special energy rituals. Each of these routines will boost your personal success, enhancing your charisma and inner strength. Enjoy feeling your life improve as you systematically tick off each of these activities.

1. SPROUT A PLANT IN THE SOUTH EAST TO BRING IN A NEW SOURCE OF INCOME

By placing sprouting plants in the South East of your home, you simulate the auspicious presence of Sheng Chi and create multiple sources of income. If there is no growth in the South East, wealth energy becomes increasingly depleted.

2. PLACE A WATER FEATURE IN THE SOUTH EAST

As you've already read, to attract serious wealth into your life, choose a substantial sized water feature, ie; a pool or fishpond dug into the ground in the South East part of your garden. This activates an extremely powerful way to attract abundance luck to the family.

3. HANG A MANDALA ON YOUR SOUTH WALL

Mandalas reflect the powerful energies of heaven and Earth, which can then combine with the energy of the people in the home. This forms a powerful trinity in Feng Shui. A beautiful and well-drawn Mandala will ensure your house is properly safeguarded and will also encourage good health for all residents.

4. THROW A PARTY ON A SPECIAL DAY

It is always good to bring a blast of Yang energy into your home. Invite a group of friends who care for you, whose auras glow with good will for you, and who are happy to come together in celebration with you. Good Feng Shui parties will dissolve any negative energy that has become stuck in your home, transforming it in to positive Chi.

5. ALLOW YANG ENERGY INTO THE FACING PALACE OF YOUR HOME

The facing palace is the part of the house where Chi enters and distributes. Make sure it is clutter-free and brightly lit. Place Fu Dogs at your front door entrance to guard your home from any harmful energy entering.

6. ENERGISE A ROOM WITH THE SUN AND MOON SIGN

The signs of the Sun and Moon have an empowering energy when combined. It also signifies the balance of Yin and Yang. Place this symbol in your home to activate their special energy.

7. WEAR THE WISH-FULFILLING MANTRA RING

Wear the wish-fulfilling mantra ring on any finger to create a protective aura and defend against negative vibes. It helps you achieve your desires when worn. Your goals can be for spiritual, emotional, mental, physical and material fulfilment. You can also wear the mantra ring on a chain around your neck.

8. FIRE UP YOUR LOVE LIFE WITH PEACH BLOSSOM LUCK

Peach blossom luck is a Feng Shui formula that can be applied when one is looking for love. You can identify your personal peach blossom animal from your Chinese Astrology animal sign, which is ascertained from your year of birth. Your peach blossom animal will be either the Horse, Rooster, Rabbit or Rat depending on your animal sign. Place a symbol of your peach blossom animal in a prominent place in its corresponding part of the house. This will energise your love life with new possibilities.

9. PLACE A METAL FEATURE IN THE NORTH WEST

Protect the luck of the family's breadwinner by placing metal in the North West. You can also use a metallic sculpture of your choice if that is your preference, however, ensure the sculpture you use is non-threatening and without poison arrows. The North West is the symbolic place of the father or leader of your house, and if he does well, so will the entire family by extension.

10. PLACE A PAINTING OF 100 BIRDS OUTSIDE YOUR FRONT DOOR

Birds symbolise a variety of opportunities that have the potential to change one's life for the better. They bring good news in to the home.
The more birds the better and it doesn't matter what type they are, although colourful plumage is particularly auspicious.

11. PLACE SEA SALT OR ROCK SALT INSIDE YOUR WALLET TO ATTRACT CASH LUCK

Sea salt has great cleansing properties and also has the capacity to attract wealth. Sewing several grains of sea salt into a small pouch in your wallet will attract cash in to it and ensure money doesn't leave your wallet.

12. CREATE AN AQUARIUM FILLED WITH LITTLE FISH FOR CAREER LUCK

To boost you career luck, activate the North section in your home with an aquarium and ensure it is properly maintained. Swimming fish provide a constant source of Yang energy in the North sector.

AFFLICTIONS AND CURSES

THREE DOORS IN A ROW

When there are too many doors in a row, it symbolises too many mouths in the household. This creates bickering and fighting. It also causes the Chi to flow too fast through the house, forming a poison arrow. Rooms at the end of a corridor with three doors in a row will suffer ill health.

THE CURE

Hang faceted crystal balls, or a Mayan Ball, on top of the doorways; these will dissolve the fast moving Sha Chi shooting through the corridor. You can also use screens to block off the doors from each other. These force the energies to slow down and meander rather than shoot through your house.

CENTIPEDE ARRANGEMENT

Many offices, especially those trying to economise on floor space, have desks arranged so they form what is known as the 'centipede' arrangement. This causes bickering and petty politics in the workplace. If you are placed within such a centipede and you are sitting facing one of your inauspicious directions, you will be on the receiving end of 'office politics'.

THE CURE

Display a figurine of a Rooster on your desk to control the centipede. Also, energise the mentor corner (North West) of your desk with an Amethyst gemstone. As well as improving your relations with others in the office, a gemstone in the North West will gain you the support of your boss.

OVERHEAD BEAMS

Overhead beams, as far as possible, should not be exposed. When exposed, they hurt the Chi of the family and are an obstacle to growth and wealth accumulation. When chairs, desks or beds are placed below an overhead beam, they cause headaches, ill health, bad luck and problems in business.

THE CURE

The best remedy for such beams would be to create a false ceiling to hide the beams. If this is not possible (for example, if it would make the ceiling too low, which again is bad Feng Shui), use a crystal or Bamboo Flutes.

SYMBOLISM

HANG A PICTURE OF A SUNRISE IN THE SOUTH

The South is the place of new opportunities. A picture of a sunrise in this corner of your living room will open up bright new avenues for growth in your life.

ACTIVATE THE WEALTH CORNER OF YOUR LIVING AREA

The wealth corner is the South East. Energise this corner by placing a leafy green plant or a bubbling aquarium there. Do not do this in bedrooms, toilets or dining areas.

GROW CUMQUATS, ORANGES OR LIMES

The ripening of fruit symbolises good fortune and prosperity. Display them at the entrance of your home.

PLACE STEREO AND TV EQUIPMENT ON THE WEST WALL

All stereo and hi-fi equipment brings extra family and descendant luck to the house when placed on the West wall of the living room.

YIN AND YANG IN THE COSMIC BALANCE

All the energies of your personal space are in a constant state of flux. Yin and Yang energies dance together continually - striving for the balance that brings harmony. Yin is cool, dark and lifeless - still. Yang is hot, bright and full of life. Keep Yin and Yang in harmony within your home and you will enjoy good luck.

REGULAR SHAPES ARE BETTER

Regular shapes are preferred to irregular shapes. Squares and rectangles have better Feng Shui than triangles or shapes with missing corners.

CURVED PATHWAYS BRING BETTER LUCK

Any pathways that lead to your front door are best to meander, thereby slowing down the energy that brings good fortune.

BEWARE OF STRAIGHT ROADS

Front doors should not face oncoming roads, eg; t-junctions and end of streets. Slow down the energy by planting a row of trees with good foliage so that the on-coming road is 'blocked off'; build a wall that effectively closes off the view of the offending road; and hang a Convex Bagua mirror outside to ward off the Sha Chi and prevent it from entering your home.

OPEN WINDOWS

Open windows in each room at least once a week, in order to move stale air and bring in fresh Yang air and energy to attract good fortune.

FRESH FLOWERS

Fresh flowers are great Yang energy. Never leave dying withering flowers, always discard them immediately.

ARTIFICIAL FLOWERS VERSUS DRIED FLOWERS

Dried flowers are not considered auspicious as they can undermine your success. Artificial silk or plastic is preferable.

DISPLAY PEONIES FOR LOVE

The peony – 'the king of flowers' – is a symbol of good fortune associated with women and romance. It is believed the peony keeps love and romance alive.

TO ENHANCE ROMANCE AND RELATIONSHIP LUCK

To enhance romance and encourage love, passion and companionship, keep something symbolic of love and romance in the South West section of your home, or South West section of your bedroom. The best thing to place is a pair of Mandarin Ducks in this area. Ducks symbolise fidelity and happiness.

Some alternatives are;
- Anything heart shaped or in pairs, eg; red candles, happy pictures of you as a couple
- Romantic or erotic pictures
- Sensual figurines
- Sculpture of man and woman in loving embrace
- Six smooth crystal balls – place six crystal balls in the South West corner of the bedroom or living area for love and a steady relationship

FOR THE MAIN BEDROOM
- Never put plants or flowers in the bedroom
- Fruit is excellent in the bedroom, especially the pomegranate as it is a symbol of fertility
- Decorate your bedroom in red during the early years of your relationship. If red is too strong use pink or peach. Red represents passion and strong Yang energy, and brings luck to those wanting children
- Avoid mirrors if possible
- Avoid a TV if possible
- Avoid anything that suggests water.
- In the next chapter we take a look at tips for romance and love in more depth.

PLANT A JADE TREE

Plants have special symbolism in Feng Shui. The Jade tree is the ultimate symbol of prosperity for the Chinese. Its flat round leaves and compact shape makes it the Asian equivalent of a money tree.

It is a succulent which cannot tolerate over-watering. It rarely flowers indoors, but if given the right conditions it can produce tiny star like flowers which are white/pink in colour. As a houseplant it resembles miniature trees and requires good light to grow. Allow the soil to dry completely in-between watering. Under-watered succulents will have 'crinkled' leaves and over-watered ones will have leaves soft and yellow, and start to drop off.

Bury Chinese Coins in the soil of the plant and place in the wealth corner of your office or home. Buy two or three plants and place in the same area or at the front and back doors of your home. Symbolically, as the plant grows so too will abundance in your life.

SYMBOLISM OF PLANTS AND OBJECTS

Acacia Tree: Permanence
Apricot: Fruitfulness
Aspidistra: Fortitude
Bamboo: Youth, perseverance and good luck
Bats: Good fortune
Bear: Strength and courage, protection against theft
Begonia: Perfect Yin/Yang balance
Bird: Happiness
Black water: Wisdom
Blue: Heavenly
Camellia: Evergreen
Cherry: Fruitfulness
Chrysanthemum: Endurance and long life
Coins: Prosperity
Clouds: Heavenly blessings
Conch shell: Prosperity
Cranes: Loyalty, long life
Cypress: Nobility
Deer: Good luck and wealth
Delphinium: Consolation
Dog: Prosperity and protection
Dragon: Strength and authority
Elephant: Strength and wisdom
Fish: Success and plenty
Flowers: Wealth
Gardenia: Strength
Gold: Wealth
Hibiscus: Profusion
Horse: Endurance
House unity: Good fortune
Hydrangea: Achievement
Jade: Wealth
Jasmine: Friendship

Juniper: Tolerance
Lilies: Profusion
Lion: Strength and majesty
Lotus: Perseverance
Magnolia: Fragrance
Mountains: Strength, endurance
Old Man: Longevity
Orange: Wealth
Orchid: Patience and endurance
Peach: Friendship
Pear: Long life
Peony: Wealth
Pine Tree: Longevity
Phoenix: Gracefulness and wisdom
Plum: Beauty and youth
Pomegranate: Fertility
Red Happiness: Prosperity
Rhododendron: Delicacy
Rocks: Endurance
Sky: Heavenly blessings
Sun: Health and happiness
Swallows: Prosperity and success
Tiger: Strength and stamina
Toad: Wealth
Tortoise shell: Longevity
Two goldfish: Success and abundance
Unicorn: Power and position
Vase: Peacefulness
Water lily: Fortitude
Willow: Grace
Wisteria: Beauty
White: Purity
Yellow: Purity

ROMANCE LUCK

The Chinese believe that in every woman's lifetime she has several opportunities of marriage, and that each of these opportunities represents a crossroad. Some of these opportunities are stronger than others, and some represent a better future than others.

These opportunities are part of her heaven luck (heaven luck is your fate; the luck you were born with). How and what she makes of these opportunities depend on her Earth luck and her man luck.

It is in this context that Feng Shui can be of some help. Feng Shui is the manifestation of Earth luck, and if a woman can knowingly arrange her living surroundings in such a way as to promote auspicious luck in the area of romance, marriage and family alike, she will have improved her chances of achieving happiness in a good marriage that leads to a happy and contented family life.

For men, romance and marriage luck also work in the same way, but readers must understand that Chinese cultural tradition accepts the arrangement of multiple wives and concubines. To the Chinese mind, marital arrangements comprise the chief wife and also secondary wives. Thus, it is the number one wife who is recognised as the head woman of the household – but there is also room for secondary wives, and even for mistresses.

In modern day Chinese households, especially those of Chinese who have lived in Western cultures for generations, much of this tradition is considered nonsense. Nevertheless, understanding the benefits of tapping Feng Shui luck, must be seen in this context.

Good marriage luck for women indicates she will become a happy first wife, and that even if the husband strays, or has a wandering eye, he will continue to respect and provide for his first wife, and that his children by her will take precedence at all family occasions.

Part of both Form School and Bagua School Feng Shui, women are strenuously advised against having mirrors in the bedrooms, having a fish pond or aquarium on the right hand side of the main door of their homes, or having a toilet located in the marriage or family corners of the home.

In addition, where there is good Feng Shui, auspicious and balanced Chi also brings about balance into the physical bodies of individuals, thereby promoting good health and a general absence of illnesses and disease.

To activate your marriage section and increase the chances of serious romance in to your life, locate the South West. It's best if your toilet, bathroom or kitchen are not located in the South West section.

Toilets are especially harmful, since this literally means flushing away all your marriage prospects. If you find you have a toilet placed in the South West section of your home, and there is nothing you can do about it, then stop using this toilet altogether. If you are already married and you perceive your marriage to be in trouble, this may be the cause. When toilets are located in the marriage section, marriages tend to get into trouble. Having toilets located in the family section can also cause family problems. This is the East section of the house. Readers will find that every section of the home represents one of the desirable aspirations of living, and it is up to each reader to decide what is most important in his/her life.

One might well ask then, where the toilets of a home can be located, since placing it anywhere seems to cause problems of one kind or another.

This depends on the individual. It is perhaps interesting to note that in the palaces and homes of the wealthy Mandarins of olden China, there were no toilets. Nor were there bathrooms. These are modern day creations of Western cultures. In the olden days, bathtubs were filled with water by servants and maids, and then taken away each time the master or mistress needed a bath. Other bodily ablutions were handled the same way. If your South West corner is missing, due to the shape of your home or apartment, this can also cause marriage problems. The solution is to erect a wall to extend out the corner, thereby apparently creating space in the South West section.

It's possible to activate the marriage section, vastly improving one's marriage prospects. This is done by hanging a red Chinese marriage knot in the South West section, or hanging the Chinese characters signifying double happiness (a symbol of conjugal bliss).

TIPS TO ATTRACT LOVE AND ROMANCE

If you are looking for someone special, here are some general Feng Shui tips to attract love and romance into your life:

- As the South West section of your home is the relationship sector, ensure there is no clutter in this area of your house
- In the South West section of your bedroom set aside a small area to dedicate to the kind of relationship you are looking for. Place Mandarin Ducks, crystals, candles, paintings, postcards or prints that symbolise a happy relationship there. If you are looking for someone who is affectionate, ensure the images you have chosen show a couple holding hands, or hugging each other. Every time you see this area, say a positive affirmation such as, 'I have a wonderful loving relationship'
- Take some time to write down the type of person you are looking for. Be specific and don't leave anything out. Place the profile of your perfect partner under the products you have placed in the South West section.
- Ensure furniture is paired in the bedroom. Two matching lamps, two matching side tables, two candles, etc
- Place a Double Happiness Symbol or picture in the South West section of your bedroom or home
- Place a vase of Peonies in the home
- Place a beautiful, romantic picture or print on the wall, or a photo frame of you and your partner in the South West section of your bedroom or home. Photos of family members or children should be placed in the West area of your home as this sector relates to family relationships
- The most important thing to do, is to go out and date. Mr or Mrs Right is not going to come knocking on your door. A little effort is required to make your dreams come true!

FACE READING

HELPFUL TIPS IN LOOKING FOR YOUR IDEAL PARTNER

IF YOU'RE LOOKING FOR A MAN

Look for a man who has a broad, fleshy and tall nose supported by a pair of decent cheeks which are fleshy and prominent, but not overly protruding nor bony, is a partner who is (or will be) rich enough and able to provide a life of financial ease and support.

A man with a spacious forehead (without bumps, indentation or scars) of at least four finger spaces, is a man who can command considerable authority and can rise up the ranks of a civil or corporate career.

However, these qualities alone may not give you a man who can easily share emotions and communicate with you 'on the same level'. For this, you're looking for a man with expressive eyes, which are not too small and with double eyelids. Additionally, check his mouth, you're looking for a mouth that is well-defined with clear borders and with a decent upper lip that is not too thin and preferably balanced with the lower lip.

IF YOU'RE LOOKING FOR A LADY

For success for yourself, both financially and in your career, then your ideal woman should have a well-defined nose that would 'prosper' her husband. A woman's nose is the prime indicator of the potential achievement of her man, particularly with the modern indicators of success, career and wealth. A good nose of a lady who marries well, should be tall and with a decent nose bridge. Similarly, the candidate in question should also have adequate cheeks which support the nose.

A woman with very high and prominent cheek bones is bound to have strong opinions and make her own decisions. These characteristics make a good corporate woman and one who can also 'bring home the bacon', so to speak.

While large, glassy eyes with double eyelids can make your anima fantasies come true, they also make for a lady who is very emotional. These type of eyes belong to a lady who will likely share with you her every thought, feeling, fear and paranoia. If you're the kind who's easily dragged down by constant nagging and sharing of thoughts and feelings, stick to someone whose eyes are not overly large or watery.

TIPS TO BOOST EDUCATION LUCK

If you're looking at enhancing your luck on an educational level, here are some tips to help you on your way.

NORTH EAST FOR EDUCATION LUCK

The North East sector governs education luck and its element is Earth. If you want to achieve good grades in your studies, you should activate the North East sectors of your desk, study, bedroom and living room to boost your education luck. The best Earth element energisers are natural Quartz crystals and objects that represent the Earth element. You can also use the Fire element in the form of bright lights. Display the world map in the North East sector and keep that corner brightly lit.

CARP FOR SCHOLASTIC FINESSE

Display an image of the carp on your study desk to energise for education and knowledge luck. The auspicious carp symbolises perseverance because of its legendary valour in swimming against the current of the Yellow River. Hence, it's a fantastic energiser for scholastic finesse and superior knowledge.

GLOBE FOR ACADEMIC SUCCESS

The crystal globe is the ultimate enhancer for education, literary and scholastic luck. If you are a student, this will bring you good luck in your studies and examinations. Place it in the North East and twirl it once a day.

AMETHYST GEMSTONE FOR KNOWLEDGE

An Amethyst gemstone gives you spiritual insight coupled with intellectual reasoning. Place it on your study desk to help you focus your mental powers and develop better concentration when you study.

Amethyst is a wonderful gemstone for opening your mind to new ideas while providing common sense and encouraging flexibility in decisions. Display the Amethyst gemstone in the North East of your living room to promote the growth of knowledge.

ABACUS FOR ANALYTIC ABILITY

An abacus is an excellent energiser for students who want to excel in fields that require excellent skills in computing and analysing figures. If you need to get excellent grades in subjects like accounting, economics, computer science, mathematics or physics then you should display a brass abacus on your study desk.

PERSONAL STUDY CRYSTAL

Every student should own a personal study crystal to energise for academic achievement. Hold the facetted crystal point in your hand when you are studying and put it on the North East of your desk when you are not using it. Using a study crystal keeps you highly motivated so that you are more focused; it also improves your memory. Cleanse your crystal by soaking it for seven days and seven nights in a solution made by dissolving seven spoonfuls of sea salt or rock salt in water. Rinse it thoroughly under running tap water before you begin using it. Keep your crystal in a pouch so that no one else touches it.

LUCKY AND UNLUCKY NUMBERS

In Feng Shui, some numbers are considered lucky and some unlucky. This is because of the way the numbers sound when spoken, especially to the Cantonese. For example; 11 sounds like heaven, or eight sounds like weight, or one sounds like son.

NUMBERS CONSIDERED UNLUCKY

The number four is the most unlucky number because in Cantonese when the number four is spoken (sei), it sounds like the word death. The number 13 is unlucky because when you add one and three, it equals four. Numbers 24 and 104 are also considered unlucky.

There are many other numbers I have read about that are considered unlucky and in my opinion, this is untrue and written to fill space. If you think about it, you could go on for a while; the number four when spoken in English sounds like door, more, store, bore, jaw, paw and saw.

NUMBERS CONSIDERED LUCKY

The lucky numbers are 8, 18, 28, 38, 48, 58, 68, 80, 84, 88, 98, 108 and 168. The Chinese word for eight is 'patt'. The number eight is lucky because when saying the word 'patt', it sounds like 'faat', which means prosperity and abundance.

The numbers 2, 5, 6, 8 and 9 are also lucky; two means easy, five means in harmony with the Five Elements, six represents wealth, eight means becoming rich, and nine is synonymous with longevity. Thus, an office address such as 289 means it's easy to become rich for a long period or that the business will prosper for a long time. On the other hand, the number 744 augurs that the business will not succeed.

The Chinese prefer double digits to avoid the feeling of loneliness. Number three is not particularly lucky, even if it sounds like 'alive' in Cantonese.

CURE IF YOUR HOUSE OR BUSINESS NUMBER IS UNLUCKY

If you own a home or business with an unlucky number, the cure is as simple as drawing a circle around the number. The circle is extremely powerful and encloses the inauspicious effects of a negative number. Or, you can purchase ceramic door numbers from your local hardware store that you can customise with a circle around the number. It's seriously that easy!

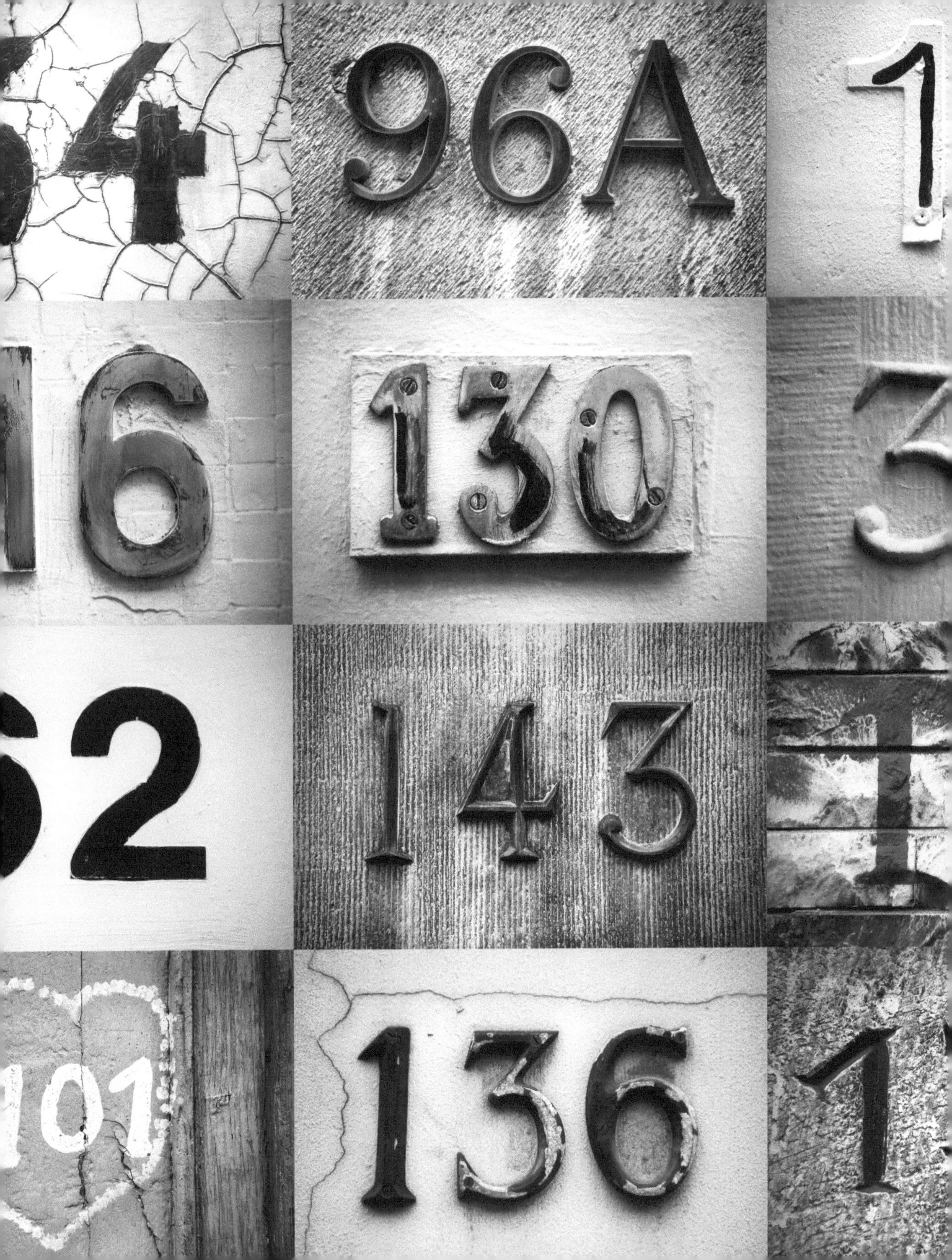
96A
130
143
136

GIFTS YOU SHOULD NEVER GIVE

Giving and receiving gifts is a wonderful exchange that shows we care. One would think that any gift given from the heart is good. Unfortunately, this is not always the case. An inauspicious gift is bad news, no matter how noble your intentions are. Taken from a Feng Shui perspective, some things are worse compared to others. Here are the top five gifts you should never give to anyone.

SHARP OBJECTS

Giving sharp objects as a gift will literally sever the friendship. As sharp objects are a natural source of Sha Chi, such gifts will result in you unintentionally sending bad luck to your friend.

Examples of sharp objects that are unsuitable as gifts include a blade, chainsaw, dagger, hunting knife, letter opener, penknife, scissors, Swiss Army knife and sword.

Fortunately, for these types of gifts there is are remedy. Ask the person you are giving the gift to, for a coin or some change (ensure it is Metal) before you present your gift to them. This simple exchange symbolises a 'purchase', instead of a 'gift'. Since your friend symbolically 'paid' for the item, in Feng Shui it is no longer considered a 'gift'. This uncomplicated remedy works only for sharp Metal items.

TIMEPIECES

In Western culture, timepieces are quite well-liked as gifts. These include an alarm clock, wall clock, pocket watch, wristwatch, etc.

Timepieces measure the passage of time and this indirectly suggests a limited lifespan which is very inauspicious. In Chinese (Cantonese), to give a clock sounds exactly like the Chinese term for attending a funeral.

RED ROSES

Long stemmed red roses with sharp thorns are terrible as gifts – it's true! The longer the stem and the sharper the thorns, the more the relationship will suffer. If you send your lover a bouquet of red roses it will be the beginning of the end of the relationship.

It is better for you to give cream or pink roses. Feng Shui-wise, yellow roses work even better to help enhance that loving feeling. Remember to have the thorns removed.

SHOES

In Chinese (Cantonese), the word for shoes (hai), sounds very much like a sigh. This is very inauspicious as it suggests much unhappiness. A gift of shoes to your friend would be akin to sending bad luck his or her way.

HANDKERCHIEFS

Gifts of handkerchiefs are also traditionally frowned upon. This is because a handkerchief is used to wipe away sweat and tears which suggests a lot of sadness and frustration. Giving handkerchiefs as gifts suggest that you anticipate the receiver to be doing much crying in the future. This generates such an inauspicious Chi.

MYTHS AND MISCONCEPTIONS

Feng Shui has many myths and misconceptions – here are some common ones.

DINING TABLE

The shape of your dining table is of little or no Feng Shui consequence. This is untrue; an eight setting table is the most auspicious which can be in a rectangular or circle shape.

Another common misconception is that a large mirror next to the dining table is auspicious as it 'doubles' the food on the table. This is somewhat far-fetched as we know that the reflection disappears as soon as real food is consumed.

T-JUNCTION

Facing a T-junction is a definite problem, but the misconception lies with the 'remedy'. Most people resort to using mirrors to 'reflect' away the incoming forceful energy flow, however, mirrors do little in this case. To rectify, ensure that your main door is not directly aligned with the road junction. Use another entrance if necessary. Next, see if you can physically block off the junction view by building a wall, or perhaps with strategic placement of solid trees (or pots of plants) to act as a physical barrier.

BRIGHT HALL EFFECT

The 'bright hall effect' refers to a broad and open space that allows energy to gather. This applies to playgrounds and gardens as well and houses situated near these open spaces. Next, you need to ensure that the area just outside your main door is spacious and unobstructed (external bright hall). This allows energy to gather outside your property. Then, ensure the area directly after your door is also relatively spacious so that energy can enter the property. Note, a bright hall does not involve making it brighter with lights nor will bright lights increase the quality of energy.

SOURCE OF YANG ENERGY

Source of Yang energy refers mainly to natural sunlight. All houses should receive a healthy dose of sunlight, as sunlight is the natural source of Yang energy. The main door for example, should be adequately exposed to natural light. Conversely, a main door that is hidden in shadows is inflicted by 'Yin Killings', meaning too much Yin energy will be attracted into the house. This often contributes to illness as well as depression. What you need to know is that Yang energy refers to natural light, and not artificial generated electricity.

COLOUR SCHEME

Colour scheme is also a subject of confusion. We all react individually to the variational energy of colour and this is because colour vibrates at different frequencies and creates a reaction in us all. The colour that emanates from your walls has the power to make you feel content, calm, or inspired. Conversely, unsuitable colours make you unsettled, restless, argumentative and can even cause ill health and loss of wealth.

Practise some common sense when planning your colour scheme. We know that too many depressive colours like black, dark blue or purple can cause a person to become too relaxed and lacking in motivation and inspiration. Too many bright colours, on the other hand, can cause over excitement and difficulty in getting good rest. Balance is the key - think Yin (deeper, sombre colours) and Yang (bright, vibrant colours) working in harmony.

BLUNDERS

The results simply refuse to come and you're on the verge of giving up – here are some common Feng Shui booby traps and how to avoid them.

GREAT EXPECTATIONS

You have watched as your best friend gets promoted, finds a partner and seems to be blooming overnight, all seemingly due to good Feng Shui. You have been secretly practicing for a couple of weeks now and life is still drab and unexciting as ever. Expecting too much, too soon, is one of the biggest Feng Shui blunders. Feng Shui is a complex practice and results are a function of different forces. Putting too intense an expectation of results can often cause obstacles to arise because of all the negative angst you are generating.

SOLUTION

Take it easy. Relaxed and steady should be your attitude. Remember that Feng Shui is about being protected against bad things happening, so when life is boring it may just be that things are moving along so smoothly that you feel bored. Think this through carefully and you might start to see how Feng Shui has already worked for you without you even realising it.

LOOKING FOR INSTANT RESULTS

When you first start Feng Shui, it is understandable that you will be on the constant lookout for fast results, constantly checking for progress. When it is love you seek, you expect to meet that special someone every day, not realising that sending out these kinds of desperate vibes has just the opposite effect. If money is what you have activated for, keeping a daily vigil for money to drop from the skies will not do the trick. Feng Shui rarely works like this.

SOLUTION

Usually, good things creep up on us without us noticing. Let your luck build up steadily and in whatever speed is in sync with your personal Chi energies. Feng Shui always brings results but the speed with which it works differs from time to time and from person to person - so put your Feng Shui in place and then let it go. Leave it to the cosmos to bring you the results you want, without you having to keep checking.

CONSULTING TOO MANY 'EXPERTS'

The kiasu attitude in all of us makes us ask too many people for their opinion. We cannot help wanting to check with anyone who claims to be an 'expert', whether what we are doing is right or wrong - assuming they must surely know. Experts know things from their own perspective and when answering your questions, often do not have the same perspective as you. When you consult too many experts, you cause yourself to get confused and this can cause you to get things mixed up. This is where problems almost always arise because the end result is an array of methods that don't work. A bit of this and a bit of that is definitely not good Feng Shui practice.

SOLUTION

The key to success is to understand exactly what you need to do, and to have confidence in yourself. Sometimes it is better to keep things simple. Never let self-styled 'experts' cause Feng Shui havoc in your home, especially when they fiddle with your directions, or even worse, cause you to undo all the good you have done. Stay the course and have faith in your own methods. Trust your gut instinct.

GETTING SIDE TRACKED

It is easy to get distracted when trying to do too many things at the same time. Better to go step-by-step. Take an organised approach and be clear of what you want to achieve. Feng Shui is a complex practice that involves design, construction, arrangement of layouts, appearance and aesthetics. It is not a straightforward matter, so try not to get side tracked. Instead, get organised and stay on course.

SOLUTION

Those who get the best results from Feng Shui are not those who know the most formulas. They are those with a clear perspective of what they want to achieve from using Feng Shui. Plan your Feng Shui practice carefully.

NOT USING A PROPER COMPASS

It's easy to take the lazy approach and 'guesstimate' the compass directions using nothing more than the direction of the sun to pinpoint specific orientations. This is one of the most common blunders that can cause your Feng Shui to go wrong. This is because good Feng Shui depends on correct orientations and you need a compass for this.

SOLUTION

Invest in a compass. Get a Lo Pan (a Feng Shui compass) if you have ambitions to be a Feng Shui consultant. Amateur practitioners need only a small compass, but it should be well made and well insulated against the magnetic fields around us. Get into the habit of taking your orientation at all times. You will get some spectacular results by tapping into your auspicious directions and avoiding your unlucky directions.

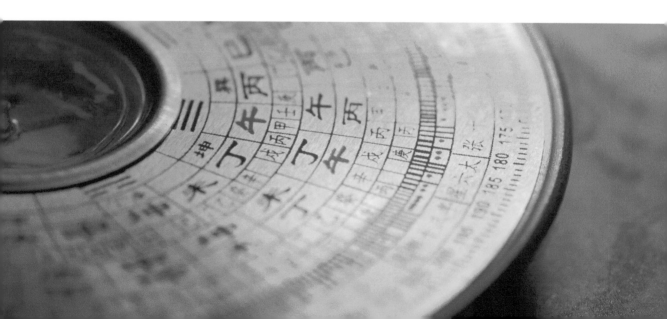

GETTING HUNG UP ON TERMINOLOGY

Feng Shui has become so popular that we are seeing plenty of opinions on what it is and how it should be practised. The danger of this is that we can get too hung up on terminology as a result, causing blunders to occur.

SOLUTION

It's best not to worry about the way Feng Shui is defined. What's important is to look at what you want to do. You can incorporate anything you want into your practice if that makes you happy. Definitions and terminologies only cloud the real practise, so rise above these things.

NOT USING CONVENTIONAL WISDOM, AKA COMMON SENSE

It's so easy to get hung up on 'expertise' that we give up on using good old common sense. Never belittle the importance of conventional wisdom. Even as we use Feng Shui, we should also use our brains.

SOLUTION

Feng Shui is about good sound, common sense and it's this that ensures everything is approached rationally – with a big dose of our personalised cultural beliefs and habits. Feng Shui must be used to serve us. It is after all, a skill – a tool for us to use with wisdom. Whenever you are in doubt about anything, ask yourself if it makes sense to you.

WEALTH VASE

One of the most interesting accessories for a Feng Shui enthusiast to include in the home is a wealth vase. This is a vase filled with personal items which are precious to the owner, that are said to attract luck.

A wealth vase used to be something only the wealthiest and noblest of families in China were privy to. Today, secrets associated with the creation of a family wealth vase have become available through the teachings of contemporary Taoist and Buddhist Masters. The practice has origins in these two major Chinese traditions, and if you visit some of the older family homes in Beijing, Shanghai or Xian, you might be able to view some magnificently huge wealth vases belonging to the noble families of another time – vases that have lasted through generations. These wealth vases were credited to bringing continuous wealth and power to families through the days of the Ching Emperors and Communist rulers, allowing their descendents to successfully weather political and economical changes.

HOW TO MAKE YOUR OWN WEALTH VASE

To make your own wealth vase, find a beautiful and preferably valuable vase to hold your precious items. The vase can be made of Earth elements or Metal, although Earth vases are more effective. Earth vases can be made from porcelain, crystal or clay; while Metal element vases can be made of copper, brass, silver or gold.

If you are designing your vase to serve as an interesting decorative item, crystal will allow you to see the items inside the vase, but any of the above materials will suffice if you can't afford a solid gold vase.

The best shape for a wealth vase is one with a wide opening that narrows to a more slender neck and then widens to a squat, sturdy body. This way, wealth energy can flow easily into the vase and then settle in the broader bottom of the vase, where it will remain and gather more wealth for years to come. The vase can be any size that you like. It must have a cover of some sort, preferably a matching lid of the same material.

To assemble your wealth vase, begin with the right attitude. Know that you are assembling your vase to bring prosperity to your family for many years to come. This is not a get-rich-quick spell; it is purely a wish for your entire family to accumulate wealth for a long time, and a desire for no member of your family to ever be poor. If you make your wealth vase with the right attitude, you are sending a signal to the universe to manifest your wishes for you. This method of making a wealth vase is very powerful.

The most essential ingredient that should go into your vase first, is the soil. The soil should be placed at the bottom, and if possible, it should be the soil from the garden of a wealthy person. This is especially lucky if you have received the soil as a gift. You want the good Chi of a wealthy home in the bottom of the vase.

Next, add three, six or nine Chinese Coins tied with red string. Then fill half of the vase with seven types of semi-precious stones such as Amethyst, Citrine, Clear Quartz, Topaz, Tiger's Eye, Malachite, Coral, Lapis Lazuli, Sodalite, Cornelian, Jade, Pearl, Jasper, Aquamarine, Crystal, Rose Quartz or Turquoise.

Then continue to top up your wealth vase with the following (or as many as possible):

- A figure of a Wealth God (can be any Wealth God you feel an affinity with)
- Five Gem Globes to signify wealth from all directions
- Assorted crystal chips to signify wealth from the Earth
- Gold bars, contemporary symbols of wealth, eg; Gold Ingot – an ancient symbol of wealth
- Faux diamonds to signify the most precious treasures
- Wish-fulfilling jewels to make all your aspirations manifest
- Semi-precious stones for accumulation of assets
- A Lock Coin to safeguard your wealth
- I Ching Coins to pacify all obstacles
- Six smooth crystal balls for harmony in the family
- A Ru Yi to signify power and management of the household.

Whatever you use to fill your vase, it should fill completely to the top. If there is still a gap at the top, fill it the rest of the way with semi-precious stones. When your vase is finished you must close it and cover it with five coloured cotton cloths (to signify the Five Elements) and tie it tight with five strings of the five colours. The order of the coloured cloths should be blue at the bottom, followed by green, red, yellow and with white at the top. Ensure you have the correct order of colours. Then, use the five coloured threads to tie the cloth at the neck of the vase. Braid the extra thread together and use cellophane tape (or something else you might prefer) to stick the end of the braid together.

If you have used an Earth element vase, place it in the South West or North East section of your home. If you used a Metal vase, place it in the West or North West section. The vase should be kept somewhere away from where others can see it, and never facing the front door, as this will drain the wealth luck from the vase. The best place to store your wealth vase is the inside of your cupboard in your own bedroom.

SALT WATER CURE

A salt water cure is a popular Feng Shui cure used to neutralise the potentially negative effects of challenging Feng Shui in a home and office.

The salt water cure is considered a powerful cure because salt is an ancient mineral with precious properties including strong cleansing properties, and it has been used in various cleansing rituals since very old times. Salt is also used in various body purification treatments and massages as it has the ability to absorb the negative, dull, low energies, thus leaving the energy fresh and pure.

In simple terms, the salt water cure combines the strong purifying effects of salt and water, combined with the chemical reaction between Metal and salt (the Metal element is present in this cure with the use of Chinese Coins).

The look of this cure will change in time, especially if there is a lot of negative energy in the space. The container will have a build-up of salt crystals overflowing its edges and in some cases quite a thick build-up – because of this it's very common to change this cure more than once a year.

STEP-BY-STEP INSTRUCTIONS

Items you need are; salt (ideally high quality rock salt), a container (glass, porcelain or metal – something not precious as it needs to be thrown out at the end), six Chinese Coins (made from brass), water, a protective mat or a stand.

1. Fill your chosen container with salt up to 3/4 of its capacity.
2. Place the six Chinese Coins on top of the salt; the coins should be placed with the Yang side up (the side with the four Chinese characters). The use of six coins is based on the fact that in Feng Shui, six is considered to be a number with strong Metal essence.
3. Add water to fill the container to the top.
4. Place the container on a protective mat or stand, in the home area where you need it.
5. The salt water cure container should be left open, do not cover it or place it in a covered space such as a kitchen cupboard.

PLACEMENT SUGGESTIONS

Place your salt water cure in an area where you know the container will be safe, ie; not tipped over, moved or otherwise tampered with. Usually, the corner of a room works well. If you don't like the look of the salt water cure (and bear in mind it will change even more in time), place it behind a decor object so that it's not visible. For example, you can have your salt water cure behind the sofa, a screen or a big lush plant. You should have access to you salt water cure in order to add water as needed.

DISPOSING OF YOUR SALT WATER CURE

The salt water cure will absorb and accumulate a lot of negative energy, so care should be taken with its disposal. It is to be discarded after a specific amount of time, usually after one lunar year. Salt that is used for purification is not to be consumed. Do not cleanse the bowl and the coins, the whole cure needs to be discarded in its entirety.

COMPASS READING

A compass is an essential tool used in many schools of Feng Shui, and it's also essential you learn how to use your compass properly.

THE DON'TS OF TAKING A COMPASS READING

There are many things that can alter a compass reading which may result in getting an incorrect reading:

- Do not take a compass reading near a motor vehicle of any kind
- Do not take a compass reading near anything metal; be mindful of belt buckles, mobile phones, metal pens in your hand or pockets as these will alter a reading
- Do not take a compass reading near anything electrical, especially power poles
- Do not take a compass reading standing on pebbles, pea gravel, iron ore or marble.

THE DO'S OF TAKING A COMPASS READING

To take your reading:

1. Stand just outside of your home or business, in front of the building and face the building
2. Lay your compass flat in one hand
3. Have the long part of the plastic ruler (base) section pointing away from you and the compass section closest to you
4. Ensure that the compass is straight
5. Wait for the needle to settle
6. Turn the clear circular cover (above the black ring) until the red point of the needle is right in between the two thick green lines (North)
7. Your compass reading (in degrees) is where the middle red line that runs under the compass is pointing into the degrees (black print within the circle of the compass) closest to you.

HOW TO CARE FOR YOUR COMPASS

Most compasses are quite sturdy, however, there are some things to be mindful of:

- Never put it near a magnet – this can damage the compass and render it useless
- Do not shake it, as that may dislodge the needle from its pin
- Use a case or the bag that has been provided to protect your compass.

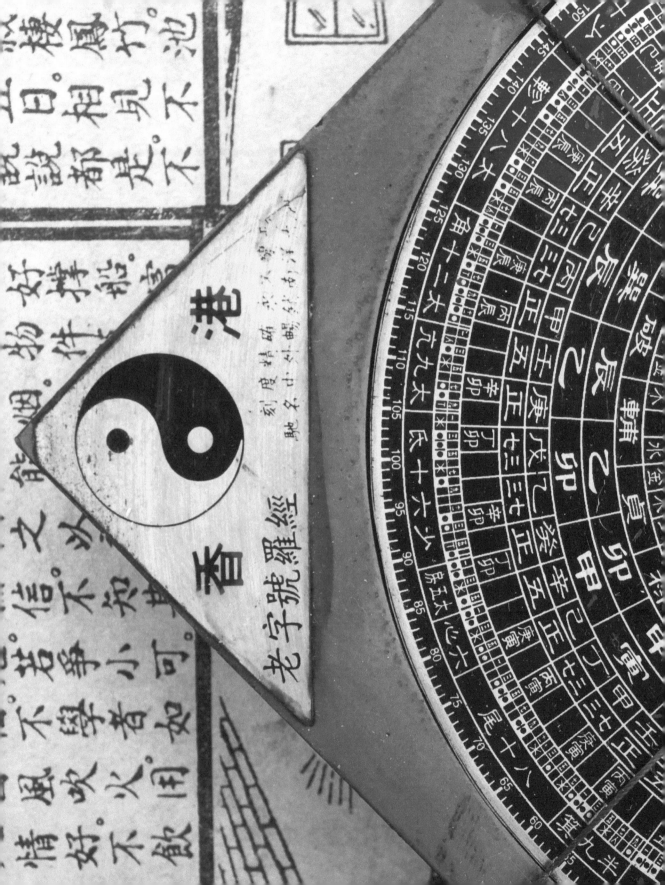

COMMON QUESTIONS

DOES FENG SHUI ALWAYS WORK?

Yes, if you get it right. Feng Shui always improves your living and work conditions, but Feng Shui is not a magic cure for every one of your problems. Remember, Feng Shui represents only one third of the trinity of luck. If you are not fated to become a big tycoon, Feng Shui may make you rich, but not seriously wealthy. That depends on your heaven luck. If your home enjoys good Feng Shui, you will find yourself becoming busier. You will be presented with opportunities to enhance your life or improve your income. You must create your own mankind luck by seizing these opportunities and accepting your good fortune.

HOW DO I KNOW IF MY HOUSE HAS BAD FENG SHUI?

You know something is wrong if you suffer a series of unfortunate occurrences shortly after moving into a new home. For example, if your family members take turns getting sick, or you lose your job for no good reason, or getting involved in an accident, or getting robbed. Bad luck can sometimes be due to your own astrological chart seeing you through a bad period, but if every person living in the same home seems to be suffering from bad luck, perhaps it might be useful to check whether something harmful is affecting the Feng Shui of your home.

HOW DO I KNOW IF AN OBJECT IS OF THE WOOD, FIRE, WATER OR METAL ELEMENT? AND IF IT IS BIG OR SMALL?

Basically, there are two ways of identifying the element energies of any object. Firstly, ask yourself what it is made of, and secondly, ask yourself what it symbolises. For instance, a Windchime made of Bamboo belongs to Wood, while one that is made of ceramic is Earth, and another made of copper or steel is Metal. In the same way, ask yourself what a globe of the world symbolises. Obviously the Earth, so it represents the Earth element. And what does a fish symbolise? Here the association is water so fish are said to symbolise the Water element. As to whether it is big or small versions of the element, here, one literally goes by size. A huge oak tree is big Wood, while a bunch of flowers is small Wood. A bridge is big Metal, while a knife is small Metal.

CAN I HAVE GOOD FENG SHUI IF I ONLY PRACTISE THE FORM SCHOOL BASICS AND IGNORE BAGUA SCHOOL ALTOGETHER?

Yes, indeed you can. You will also be able to avoid being hit by bad Feng Shui, however, Bagua School Feng Shui takes you deeper and allows you to discover powerful methods of seriously enhancing your luck. I always advise my friends to take things one step at a time. Go slowly because it is better to get the basics correct first, before trying to apply everything all at once.

HOW DO I KNOW IF THE YIN AND YANG BALANCE OF MY HOME IS CORRECT? DO I NEED TO KEEP REARRANGING MY FURNITURE EVERY TIME THE SEASON CHANGES?

When the energies of Yin and Yang are well balanced you will feel far more comfortable than if they are not. Some people call this instinctive. That may well be, however, my approach is that all Yang dwellings must have more Yang than Yin energy. The common problem is usually a shortage of Yang energy, or put another way, an excess of Yin energy is when your house is badly lit, dirty, cluttered, damp or altogether unhealthy smelling. Often, in such cases, merely opening the windows to let the sunshine in will clear the energies. Or open all the doors and windows occasionally to bring in fresh energies to replace the stale energies. As to whether you need to respond to climatic changes of the season, the answer is yes, but you don't need to rearrange your furniture. Use lights, fireplaces and fans to increase or lessen Yin and Yang energies. As with the practice of anything, there is room for creativity and initiative.

COMMON PRODUCTS

ANCIENT CHINESE COINS – have been used as a Feng Shui cure for many thousands of years and for many reasons. They symbolise wealth and they are representative of the Metal element, so can be used in areas that require this element. When placing your coins, ensure they have the side that has the four Chinese characters facing up (Yang side), which is more active than the side with the two Chinese characters (Yin side) which is more passive.

BAGUA MIRROR – is a powerful form of protection for your home or business. The trigrams are arranged in the potent heavenly sequence to protect you, your home and business from negative influences. They should never be placed within the home or business as it is too strong a cure for inside the premises and should be located on the outside of the home or business facing out. When placing, ensure that it is not being blocked by pillars, columns or the roofline/eaves.

BELLS – make a beautiful sound and are sensitive to any form of movement, making them a useful Feng Shui cure. For thousands of years bells have been symbolic of warding off negative influences and the announcement of goodwill.

BLACK TURTLE – represents longevity, strength and endurance. Place at the rear of the property to give the occupants protection and support. You may also place in the North sector to assist with career and or business.

BRASS WINDCHIMES – are used for the Metal element to assist in counteracting the negative effects of the Flying Star 5. Use also in the North West section for helpful people and mentors.

BRASS WU LU – see Precious Gourd.

DOUBLE HAPPINESS SYMBOL – represents long lasting love and strong relationships. This may be placed in the South West section of the bedroom or in the South West section of the house or office or business.

DRAGON – is one of the celestial animals in Feng Shui. A symbol of strength, courage and endurance. Place on the left hand side as you look out of the home, or the East section of a building or room to assist in the health area.

DRAGON CARP – symbolises overcoming life obstacles, encouraging success, abundance and achievement. This statue may be placed in the South East section of the home and business to assist the wealth or in the North East to assist the education and knowledge section.

DRAGON TORTOISE - is a celestial creature said to be a hybrid of the celestial dragon with the sturdy and steadfast tortoise, and is displayed by many Feng Shui practitioners to bring great fortune to their homes or workplaces. It is a powerful symbol attracting support, wealth and good luck. The Dragon brings success, and the Tortoise's longevity of tenure, ensures a long and successful career. It is a must have if you are in business or a cutthroat corporate environment. It is also a fantastic energiser for scholastic finesse and superior knowledge.

EIGHT I CHING COINS - coins for wealth used to attract good fortune and prosperity. The red pouch is used as a holder for incoming wealth luck.

NINE LEVEL PAGODA - represents literary success. Success in business dealings and peace and protection for the home.

FIVE ELEMENT PAGODA - encompasses the five essential elements of Feng Shui. This pagoda can be used to ward off negative Earth energies and of Flying Star 5.

FU DOGS - see Temple Lions.

FU LU SHOU or FUK LUK SAU - three Feng Shui Gods, respectively the God of wealth and happiness, the God of high rank and affluence, and the God of health and longevity. The Chinese strongly believe that if you place the Fuk Luk Sau in a place of prominence in your dining and living room, they will bring harmony and continuous good fortune to the household.

GOLD BAR - universal representation of gold and signify solid reserve, bypassing money notes because its value is unchallengeable. Gold bars set the fundamental baseline for world currencies from its reserve in the bank. In Feng Shui it is a strong representation of wealth, income opportunity, prosperity and abundance. This heavy gold bar is made from genuine brass.

GOLD INGOTS - called 'Yuen Bao' in Chinese. They were used as a currency by high officials and emperors in ancient China, and today in Feng Shui terms, they are regarded as the symbol of wealth and fortune. Gold Ingots are extremely auspicious and are essential ingredients for wealth vases and wealth ships. Placing them with other wealth deities such as Fuk Luk Sau and Chai Sen Yeh will magnify the effect.

HORSE - the seventh sign of the Chinese Zodiac; in Feng Shui it symbolises perseverance and strength. Horse figurines in your home or workplace will strengthen and enhance all the good traits and characteristics it represents in family members born in the year of Horse. It is no surprise that you can almost always find paintings and sculptures of horses in Chinese homes and businesses. The horses are usually classified into Tribute Horse and Victory Horse. Place in the South to enhance your reputation and to receive recognition.

I CHING COINS - to be placed in a wallet or purse, and cash register. Or in the South East section of home, office or business.

LAUGHING BUDDHA – a well-known symbol of happiness, wealth, kindness and innocent contented joy. It is believed that by rubbing his belly, which is said to contain much wealth and abundance, it will bring you good luck and prosperity. It can also bring the home or business success. He can be placed in main living areas, on desks in offices, on retail counters and reception desks. Note though, never place the Laughing Buddha directly on the floor or in negative rooms such as toilets, bathrooms or laundries.

LOCK COIN – designed to safeguard your wealth and possessions whilst enhancing your money making luck.

LUCKY KNOTS – known as the 'endless knot', used for anywhere that requires the colour red or the element of Fire.

MANDARIN DUCKS – come in pairs and are excellent symbols for keeping your love life alive. They are said to be a potent symbol of love and marital bliss as they create Chi that helps lovers tie the knot. Anyone wanting to energise their love life, should place them in the in the South West sector of your bedroom, side by side as equals. They must always be placed together, facing in and never apart.

MAYAN BALL – helps deflect negative energy and can be worn as a protective talisman. It can also be hung on windows, if you have a door opposite the window to minimise the loss of energy or Chi, and it can be hung in front of a mirror if it reflects the bed or is in line with a window.

MONEY TREE COINS – to be buried under a plant for wealth growth.

NINE EMPEROR COINS – good luck coins used to enhance the South East.

PAGODA – a temple of knowledge, peace and silence. It symbolises the path of wisdom. It is said that a person who knows more, or is knowledgeable, stands firm like a mountain or a Pagoda and cannot be shaken by anything. The Pagoda is believed to possess the power to tame unruly minds and behaviours. As you may read in many Chinese tales, the Pagoda is used for taming of cheeky spirits by 'imprisoning' them in it. Hence, it is a very useful Feng Shui enhancer and cure that brings literary luck, fame luck, protection and advancement in career. It is also potent to ward off bad energy and killing forces (Sha Chi) in your home or business. The Pagoda is a good Metal cure to use to weaken and suppress the Earth element of accidents, mishaps and losses.

PI YAO – a mythical creature of purity, loyalty, abundance and protection. The delightful Pi Yao is said to be a loyal friend who always looks after its owner. Place on your work desk, in the South East for wealth, or at your front entrance or family room.

PRECIOUS GOURD – also known as the Health Gourd or Brass Wu Lu – is an ancient Chinese symbol of longevity, protection from illness and negative energy. It can be used for promoting good health. Hang from the head of the bed or behind door. A wonderful talisman to take for travel protection.

PROSPERITY SYMBOL - a replica of the ancient Chinese Ingot; the shape being similar to a boat representing abundance and an easy life. It may be placed in the South East section of the home, office or room for attracting wealth; the West for assisting in the protection of wealth luck or in the North West section for encouraging mentors and helpful people.

QUAN YIN - known as the female Buddha, Goddess of mercy and compassion, however, she is a Goddess within her own right. She assists in deflecting conflict, arguments, disruptive issues, illness and sickness. She is also the protector of children. Quan Yin is best placed where there are disruptive issues, in a sickroom, in a child's room and open-plan offices. Note though, never place Quan Yin directly on the floor or in negative rooms such as toilets, bathrooms or laundries.

RU YI - symbolises authority and power. The Ru Yi being the sceptre for Imperial courts and offices was used by high ranking government officials including Empresses. Ru Yi has auspicious meanings; smoothness in endeavours and enhanced luck in undertakings. Ru Yi is also a potent symbol carried by Tua Peh Kong, Laughing Buddha and one of the Fuk Luk Sau (three Star Gods), resulting in enhanced wealth and abundance. The symbol is most suitably used to bring career to greater heights and raise the bar for authority. The item can be displayed to ensure we get enough control over subordinates at work and also if we have rebellious children. The Ru Yi can also protect you from evil, harmful people and misfortune.

THREE LEGGED MONEY FROG - also known as the Moon Frog - can bring prosperity to the occupants. Place the frog on the inside of the entrance of your home or business. Ensure that it is pointing into the home or business as it represents money coming into the premises; if you have the Frog pointing out it will represent money going out of the premises. If there is a stone on the coin inside the Frog's mouth, ensure that it faces up.

TEMPLE LIONS - also known as Fu Dogs - guard you from poison arrows, negative people from entering your home and also used when the 'robbery' Flying Star is located at the entrance of your premises. They are very popular in many Asian countries placed on the outside. The male is playing with a ball, he symbolises authority, courage and command. The female has her claw on her cub for protection and loyalty. Place at your front entrance, facing out with the male on the left and the female on the right.

TEN EMPEROR COINS - used to enhance the Flying Star 1 and South East.

WINDCHIME - also called Magic Bell - holds a significant presence in Feng Shui. It is without question the most powerful and versatile enhancer and cure to correct Feng Shui defects. Windchimes herald two wonderful messages; cheerfulness through the sound, and life from the wind that breathes into the tubes, and they transform bad and harmful Chi that enters your homes or office into 'Seng Chi', the intrinsic energy which brings good fortune to its occupants.

BALANCE ALL ELEMENTS
WORKING IN HARMONY
BRINGING THE OUTSIDE IN

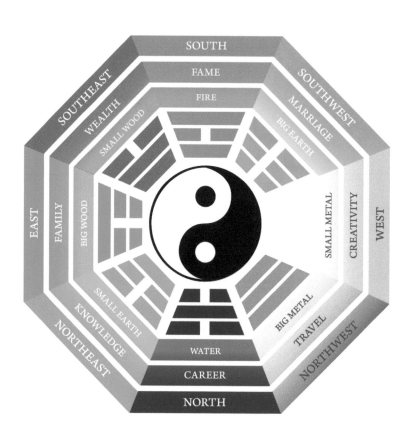

GLOSSARY

AUSPICIOUS FENG SHUI – means enjoying the eight types of Feng Shui luck. These are wealth, good health, a good family life, a long life, good luck with children, good mentors, a good reputation and a good education.

BAGUA – also called Ba-gua or Pakua – it is one of the main tools used in Feng Shui to analyse the energy of any given space, home, office or garden. Bagua is the Feng Shui energy map of your space that shows you which areas of your home or office are connected to specific areas of your life. Translated from Chinese, Bagua literally means eight areas.

BAGUA SCHOOL FENG SHUI – authentic Feng Shui practitioners always use Bagua School Feng Shui. Advanced practitioners use the Lo Pan (the Feng Shui compass) which contains many of the powerful compass formulas. Bagua combines the use of symbolism with the Bagua directions and the attributes of each room to activate the luck of Eight Aspirations. These aspirations relate to career growth, attainment of wealth, enjoying good health and family life, achieving recognition and fame, enjoying good children, attracting luck in marriage and romance, having good education luck and enjoying the patronage of powerful and influential people. Check the Flying Star natal chart prior to using this system as Flying Star overrules and you may activate the wrong type of luck. Feng Shui is based on associated directions of the compass, and by enhancing the Feng Shui in that sector of the home, potent systems for activating energy in homes, but Flying Star numbers are stronger.

BAZI – literally means 'eight characters' in Chinese. Bazi is a system of metaphysical knowledge for predicting the future of an individual. It is a very accurate and popular method used for fortune telling.

CHI – is the fundamental energy or breath found in every animate and inanimate object. An intangible force in everyone and everything. It can be positive such as Sheng Chi (growth breath) or negative such as Sha Chi (killing breath).

DESTRUCTIVE CYCLE – the cycle of elements in which Wood devours Earth, which destroys Water, which kills Fire, which consumes Metal, which destroys Wood. This cycle must be followed to ensure that the elements of objects, directions and locations in any room, do not destroy one another.

ELEMENTS – The core concept in Feng Shui practice is the theory of the Five Elements. If you understand this concept, you will become adept in Feng Shui and also gain a firm grounding in the fundamental philosophy of Chinese thought. Many Chinese things are based on the Five Elements from fortune telling (I Ching) to medical cures. The Five Elements explain the action of Feng Shui and involve a positive cycle, Wood-Fire-Earth-Metal-Water, and a negative cycle, Wood-Earth-Water-Fire-Metal.

The Five Elements theory is the foundation of all these esoteric skills. In Feng Shui, knowledge of the Five Elements theory and its cycles – productive, exhausting and destructive – offers invaluable insights into the cures, remedies and energisers recommended by Feng Shui Masters.

FLYING STARS – this is a powerful formula that reveals the transformation of luck in any living space from period to period and enables you to plan your life accordingly. This formula identifies various types of good and bad luck in the nine palaces of any home, including identifying illness and loss Stars. The nine palaces are the rooms in the home demarcated according to compass directions. The formula is based on the numbers of the Lo Shu square and it involves numerology in Feng Shui – knowing what the numbers one to nine mean and what number combinations indicate. When reading a Flying Star natal chart you will become aware of how effective Feng Shui can be. When you design your space according to the information given in these charts, at the very least, you will be protected from bad Feng Shui.

GEOMANCY – means, literally, divination by the Earth and the ground. It is a divinatory method that consists of interpreting 16 figures, each made up of four lines of points, based on Yin (even) and Yang (odd).

INAUSPICIOUS FENG SHUI – this is the opposite to auspicious Feng Shui. Most bad Feng Shui can be remedied or improved, with the appropriate cures.

KUA NUMBERS – part of the Eight Mansions formula. They are derived from a person's year of birth and gender, and are the key to determining a person's auspicious or inauspicious directions.

LO SHU SQUARE – is the three-by-three grid with nine numbers in which Feng Shui compass formulas are based.

I CHING – is the original philosophical creation of a man called Hi Fo. After combining the Yin-Yang energy in threes to form eight basic trigrams, Hi Fo then combined the eight trigrams (each made up of three Yin or Yang lines) to form 64 hexagrams (each made up of six Yin or Yang lines). Each of the hexagrams can be used in clairvoyance or teaching.

POISON ARROW – a straight or sharp structure, from which Chi bounces off at an angle, creating harmful energy.

PRODUCTIVE CYCLE - the cycle of elements in which Water feeds Wood, which feeds Fire, which makes Earth, which in-turn holds Water. This cycle must be taken into account to ensure that the elements of objects, directions and locations in any room do not destroy one another.

SHA CHI - is bad Feng Shui energy. Its Chinese translation means killing, attacking energy.

SHENG CHI - is good Feng Shui energy. It is the bright, refreshing, uplifting Feng Shui energy that is beneficial to your health and well-being. It is the only quality of energy you want to surround yourself in your home or office.

THE DRAGON EMBRACING THE TIGER - is when a subtle pattern emerges. The right side of the mountain embrace, known as the White Tiger, is always slightly higher than the left side of the mountain embrace, known as the Green Dragon. The White Tiger stands for female power whilst the Green Dragon represents male power. In classical Feng Shui there are four celestial animals:
- The Green Dragon; its hills brings abundance and prosperity
- The Crimson Phoenix; its hills represent opportunity
- The White Tiger; its hills protects
- The Black Turtle; its hills provide support.

A fundamental tenet of Feng Shui advises you to live with your back to a mountain. If your home is backed by something solid and firm such as a hill or building that stimulates the hill, you will have support all your life. Thus, the first part of classical Feng Shui is to have the mountain behind. There should be open space in front of your home, so that your vision is not hampered and your horizon is visible. If there is also a view of water, it brings auspicious energy to your living area. Moreover, if the river is slow moving and meandering, the good energy has a chance to settle and accumulate before entering your home, thereby allowing you to partake in its essence. Needless to say; the cleaner, fresher and more sparkling the water, the greater the good fortune that it will bring. Thus, the second half of classical Feng Shui says to have water in front of your home.

TRIGRAM - symbol made of broken or unbroken lines symbolising the way in which Yin and Yang combine to make Chi. There are eight trigrams and each has a different combination of broken or unbroken lines and carries different associations.

YANG - the name given to the masculine side of the energy of the universe. By extension, Yang is creative energy, the sky, the sun, the day, strength and war. This energy is symbolised by a continuous and unbroken line.

YIN - the name given to the feminine side of the energy of the universe. By extension, Yin is receptive energy, the Earth, the moon, night, passivity and woman. This energy is symbolised by a broken line.

ABOUT THE AUTHOR

Michele has been in demand as a Feng Shui consultant for more than two decades. She has been trained by Master Raymond Lo (from Hong Kong) and Juliana Abraham (from the Feng Shui Centre in Perth, Western Australia), and has studied with Dato Joey Yap and Lillian Too. Michele maintains her Master studies each year to ensure she continues to provide clients with the best of her skills. Michele has an uncanny ability to read charts and has a fantastic insight into people. She combines experience and natural intuition with the multi-layered discipline of Feng Shui, to deliver positive outcomes for clients. Michele's approach is practical, realistic and simple. She adores the reward of making a difference in the lives of her valued clients.

Having studied architectural drafting and interior design and working with interiors and renovations on her own homes it was a natural progression to incorporate Feng Shui and metaphysical studies into those projects. Applauded for her style, Michele was often asked if she could share her gift with others. Passion and dedication, combined with further studies, saw her first Feng Shui business, Energise Life Feng Shui born and evolve into Complete Feng Shui.

Michele conducts onsite Feng Shui consultations for residential and corporate clients. An accredited teacher, at recognised training institutes, author and public speaker with numerous radio and television guest appearances. Michele works alongside families, with residential homes, developers, architects, interior designers, real estate agents, restaurants, cafes, day spas and retail stores.

For any existing or proposed business client Michele can help with staff recruitment, choosing the best location and orientation for business premises, improving the atmosphere and working environment, and advisement on business stationery such as letterheads and business cards.

For the residential client, Michele offers guidance on how to improve health and harmony in the home, how to choose the best home for you and how to improve the chances of selling your home. Other services include how to choose a suitable carer for children or elderly family members and how to improve children's behaviour, sleep and studies.

Michele's practice and qualifications include Classical, Form, 8 Mansions, 24 Mountain Compass, Flying Star School Feng Shui. Site selection and design. Metaphysical studies of Four Pillars of Destiny / Bazi / Pa Chee, Qi Men, Millionaires Feng Shui with special interest and studies on Feng Shui Love and relationship luck.

Michele teaches beginner to practitioner Feng Shui seminars, workshops, courses and retreats, as well as conducting on-site learning experiences at homes and businesses. Students receive complete course notes. For those who have mastered the basics of Feng Shui and wish to continue their studies and share their knowledge with others, there are courses to explore.

With an ability to relate to people from all walks of life. Based in Perth, but regularly consulting in Singapore, Bali and eastern states of Australia on residential, business, and commercial properties.

Michele truly believes:
" Life is what our thoughts environment and energy make it".
"Change your environment and thoughts, change your life".

With the knowledge of Feng Shui, it can work to increase wealth, enhance health, and harmonise relationships.

CPSIA information can be obtained
at www.ICGtesting.com
Printed in the USA
BVHW012011030423
661674BV00001B/5